Caring for Muslim Patients

Edited by

Aziz Sheikh MRCP MRCGP DCH DRCOG DFFP

General Practitioner, Harrow
NHS R&D National Primary Care Training Fellow
Imperial College School of Medicine, London

and

Abdul Rashid Gatrad PhD FRCP FRCPCH

Consultant Paediatrician, Manor Hospital, Walsall
Honorary Senior Lecturer, University of Birmingham
Honorary Assistant Professor, University of Kentucky

Foreword by

Sir Alexander Macara

Radcliffe Medical Press Ltd
18 Marcham Road, Abingdon, Oxon OX14 1AA

British Library Cataloguing in Publication Data

A catalogue record for this book is available from the British Library.

ISBN 1 85775 372 0

Typeset by Multiplex Medway Ltd, Walderslade, Kent
Printed and bound by TJ International Ltd, Padstow, Cornwall

Contents

Foreword   v

Preface   vii

List of contributors   ix

Acknowledgements   x

Introduction   xii

Section 1:   Islam and Muslims – an overview

1   **Muslims in Britain: demographic and socio-economic position**   3
Muhammad Anwar

2   **The Muslim grand narrative**   17
Tim J Winter

3   **Health and disease: an Islamic framework**   29
Abdul Aziz Ahmed

Section 2:   The Muslim patient

4   **The family: predicament and promise**   43
Sangeeta Dhami and Aziz Sheikh

5   **Birth customs: meaning and significance**   57
Abdul Rashid Gatrad and Aziz Sheikh

6   **Managing the fasting patient: sacred ritual, modern challenges**   73
Ahmed Sadiq

7   **Hajj: journey of a lifetime**   89
       Aziz Sheikh and Abdul Rashid Gatrad

8   **Death and bereavement: an exploration**   97
       and a meditation
       Aziz Sheikh and Abdul Rashid Gatrad

9   **Conclusions: breaking barriers,**   111
       building bridges
       Aziz Sheikh and Abdul Rashid Gatrad

Section 3:   Appendices and Glossary

Appendix 1:   Islam and medicine on the   121
              World Wide Web
              Matlub Hussain

Appendix 2:   Muslim organisations   129
              Matlub Hussain and Sangeeta Dhami

Glossary   133

Index   137

Foreword

Three years ago I had the privilege of chairing a multi-faith Working Group concerned with the healthcare needs of people from ethnic minorities in the United Kingdom. It quickly became clear that the outstanding need was for education of healthcare professionals to complement the enlightened initiatives being planned by the Department of Health. We conducted a survey of medical schools, which revealed that there was limited explicit or specific cross-cultural content in curricula at any stage. The Working Party made a number of appropriate recommendations. I should not be surprised if this book were to achieve more than my Working Party did in persuading healthcare professionals, and their teachers, of the need and value of cross-cultural education informed by an 'insider's feel'.

The National Health Service has a responsibility to provide healthcare for the whole population, with a focus on each unique individual. The message of this book is that both knowledge and insight are required to combat institutional racism, whether admitted or unconscious, and to cater positively for patients with a wide diversity of beliefs and practices in a multi-cultural society.

It was a shock to realise that although Muslims represent some 20% of the world's population, of whom almost two million are British citizens, and despite a Muslim presence in the United Kingdom stretching back hundreds of years, the rest of the population, including those responsible for their health and education, know little about the religion or its adherents. Ignorance is cause enough for concern; prejudice nurtured by stereotyped misconceptions and fostered by misrepresentation is worse by far. For example, the misconception that Islam is some kind of alien Eastern religion exclusively synonymous with Asia, or that it is a creed of intolerance and subversive fundamentalism which denigrates women, are fuelled by selective publicity given to those wretched 'Islamic' regimes whose oppressive power-hungry hierarchies can be seen as a blasphemy against 'the way of peace'.

Against this discouraging background, the authors could have been forgiven for penning a plaint against prejudice. Commendably, however, they seek to 'describe what it means to belong to a sacred tradition, to explore the intricate connections between faith and health for Muslims, and consider some of the implications of this relationship for those striving to deliver culturally competent and sensitive care'. Like the Muslim vision of the tripartite nature of man 'comprising spiritus, anima and corpus, and one in which unity reigns supreme', this book falls into three interwoven parts: an overview of Islam and its adherents, with particular reference to the United Kingdom; the Muslim patient on the earthly sojourn from birth to death; and informative appendices, including a full glossary. Throughout, the hallmarks of this 'exploration of the interface between faith and health' are restraint of expression and balance of content.

Believers in any faith, for whom life is sacred and living a sacred trust – notably the monotheistic religions – will revel in the contemplation of parallels, the similarities and differences between their beliefs and those expressed in this work. The elegant and scholarly text is a joy to read; as revelation succeeds revelation preconceptions are challenged, misconceptions are aborted, and the dawn of enlightenment stirs conviction that believers and non-believers alike must do what they can to respond as fellow human beings, especially those with the privileged responsibility of a doctor or other healthcare professional. In an increasingly secular society, whose traditional values nevertheless continue to be based upon its Judeo-Christian heritage, this work might well form a model for revisiting the relationship between faith and health for those older siblings of Islam.

The Editors sound a valedictory challenge to the more cynical reader when they write, 'evidence points in favour of religious practice being associated with a diverse array of health benefits, such as better obstetric outcome, lower blood pressure, reduced risk of cancer and increased overall life expectancy'.

And peace of mind?

Sir Alexander Macara
February 2000

Preface

To protect and enhance human life and well being is part of the trust (Arabic: amanah) which each human being carries. In the world of medicine and healthcare, some of the most dramatic and awesome advances in knowledge and technology in recent years have brought relief and opportunities for a better quality of life to many. Despite this, and startling advances in communication, many aspects of human culture, values and lifestyles often remain ignored or misunderstood in the provision of healthcare. This is why this work assumes a special significance.

The doctors and healthcare personnel who have felt the need for this publication are among a growing body of professionals who realise that healthcare involves looking after the needs of the whole human being. Many of these are leading professionals in their respective fields. Their work reflects the objective of The Muslim Council of Britain (in the formation of which they have and continue to play an active role) to work for the common good and well being of society as a whole, and for a more enlightened appreciation of Islam.

The Muslim Council of Britain was established in 1997, following extensive, nationwide consultation within the Muslim community, providing a conduit to enable Muslims to contribute to Britain and British society fully. One of our priorities, guided by our membership, has been to influence healthcare practice and delivery so that it better meets the ethical concerns and the needs of those who live by a sacred vision of the world.

Among British Muslims, religion is seen as the indispensable framework within which to conduct their day-to-day life. It provides meaning, a direction and a context within which to face the many challenges inherent in living as a faith community in pluralist Britain. This framework encompasses matters relating to the family, questions of ethics and morality, and, most important of all in the context of the present work, the Muslim's understanding of health and ill health.

Of course, our overarching concern is with the health of the nation, with the values and lifestyles that impact, often powerfully and negatively, on people's health, and the size of the NHS budget. There is, for example, the need for all people to pay more attention to proper diet and adequate exercise, to enjoy the abundant facilities for outdoor pursuits and recreation, and to avoid the dominant culture of consuming harmful and destructive substances such as alcohol and tobacco.

The Muslim Council of Britain is pleased to be associated with this timely publication. We wish to record our sincere appreciation to the Editors, Dr Aziz Sheikh and Dr Abdul Rashid Gatrad, for their foresight and dedication in putting together this work. With contributions from other respected experts, this work articulates concerns of the Muslim patient which many were either unaware of or which hitherto went unrecognised. Sensitive and constructive in its approach, this book will surely be welcomed by health professionals in training and in practice.

We wish this book every success and commend it to healthcare professionals and those involved in healthcare policy and research both here in Britain and abroad.

Iqbal AKM Sacranie OBE
Secretary General
The Muslim Council of Britain
February 2000

List of contributors

Abdul Aziz Ahmed   Principal, The Iqra Academy, Glasgow.

Muhammad Anwar   Research Professor, Centre for Research in Ethnic Relations, University of Warwick, Coventry.

Sangeeta Dhami   General Practitioner, GP Direct, Harrow, Middlesex.

Abdul Rashid Gatrad   Consultant Paediatrician, Manor Hospital, Walsall, Honorary Senior Lecturer, Birmingham University, Birmingham, and Honorary Assistant Professor, University of Kentucky, USA.

Matlub Hussain   Locum ENT Surgeon, Lincoln County Hospital, Lincoln.

Sir Alexander Macara   Chairman of the UK Public Health Medicine Consultative Committee, and former Chairman of the British Medical Association Council.

Iqbal Sacranie OBE   Secretary General, Muslim Council of Britain.

Ahmed Sadiq   Consultant Ophthalmic Surgeon, Manchester Royal Eye Hospital, Manchester, Honorary Clinical Lecturer, University of Manchester, Manchester, and Adviser, Health and Medical Board, Muslim Council of Britain.

Aziz Sheikh   General Practitioner, Harrow, and NHS R&D National Primary Care Training Fellow, Imperial College School of Medicine, London.

Tim J Winter   Lecturer, School of Divinity, University of Cambridge, Cambridge.

Acknowledgements

We owe numerous debts – spiritual, material, intellectual and emotional – to the very many people who have contributed to our understanding of the ideas discussed in this work. The debts owed to these individuals we gratefully acknowledge, and we hope that through the pages that follow, they will recognise some portion of their labour, energies, vision, encouragement and support.

Co-ordinating the production of a multi-author work involves considerable co-operation between the editors, contributors, referees and publishers. Our co-authors, chosen primarily because of their in-depth involvement and understanding of the day-to-day affairs of the British Muslim community, took precious time away from their busy professional, social and family commitments to attend to our demands, and also in many instances to review the work of their fellow contributors. Many others have very kindly reviewed commented and, through their suggestions and criticisms, improved upon earlier drafts of chapters. Though far too many to mention individually, we would in particular like to thank: Dr Jane Bradley, Dr Brian Briggs, Gloria Daley, Suma Din, Professor George Freeman, Asad Hamid, Dr Sarah Hartley, Professor Brian Hurwitz, Riffat Islam, Lesley-Anne Pratchett, Dr John Salinsky, Dr Iftikhar Saraf and Dr Sarah Scambler. Our publishers, Radcliffe Medical Press, have also been supportive and efficient throughout the long gestation period of this book.

Much of our contribution has been made in that prized period of time between work and sleep, at weekends and during vacations. To our families, immediate and extended, we express our heartfelt gratitude for not only have they patiently coped with our divided attentions, but also they have, in every sense, supported, encouraged and shared in our endeavours.

Ultimately we recognise that *All praise is for Allah, Lord of all the Worlds*.

When you were born, everyone was smiling
but you were crying.
Live such a life that, when you depart, everyone is weeping
but you are smiling.

Sa'di of Shiraz (d. 1292)

Introduction

As clinicians who live and work in areas with significant Muslim communities – *of which we are a part* – it is clear that much can be done to improve the experience of healthcare for Muslim patients. Most important of all, we believe, is the recognition that patients, irrespective of their religious or cultural affiliation, have a right to be *heard*, their perspectives and world-view respected. *Caring for Muslim Patients* has been written to begin to address this concern. It seeks to describe what it means to belong to a sacred tradition, to explore the intricate connections between faith and health for Muslims, and consider some of the implications of this relationship for those striving to deliver culturally competent and sensitive healthcare.

Some 50 years after the establishment of the National Health Service (NHS), arguably one of our most humane institutions, it is noteworthy that the NHS has found it difficult to adapt to the needs of minority groups. Created historically to serve the needs of a white, culturally homogenous population, it now faces the challenge of catering for the tapestry of beliefs and cultures found in our society. Minority groups in Britain have traditionally been thought of in terms of race and, more recently, ethnicity, and there is now an important body of research and literature devoted to understanding the health needs of the principal ethnic groups. Whilst such a framework has proved extremely useful, it is, however, inadequate to describe fully the richness and complexity of pluralist Britain. We are beginning to understand the strong association between deprivation and ill health, for example. It is now clear that the 'deprived' have particular health needs that need to be realised and addressed. Another important framework for seeking to understand individuals and communities is on the basis of creed or religious affiliation. This was recognised by The European Convention of Human Rights in 1950, when it sought to guarantee individuals 'the right to freedom of thought, conscience, and religion'. That religious affiliation can affect perspectives on health, access to healthcare, and the quality and quantity of healthcare received, is slowly being recognised by those trained in the secular biomedical model.

There has existed a Muslim presence in Britain for over four centuries, yet despite this lengthy interaction Islam remains something of an enigma. The stereotype that Islam is a faith of intolerance, terrorism and fundamentalism abound in the popular press, whilst it is surprisingly common for those involved with health policy and delivery to think of Muslims as synonymous with Asians. Positions such as these reflect a profound misunderstanding of Muslims and Muslim society. Muslim numbers are globally estimated to exceed 1.2 billion, with communities found in each and every country. One such community is in Britain. It is then a matter of some importance to understand and appreciate the values and beliefs of so large and influential a segment of the human race, and the 1.5–2 million people who have made their homes in these isles. From our personal experiences, both as the providers and recipients of care, we can say with confidence that such understanding and appreciation is crucial to *connecting* and the inter-related notions of empathy, trust and respect.

The British Muslim community is heterogeneous in many respects – in terms of dress, diet, language and ethnic origin. Such diversity is recognised and indeed encouraged in Muslim culture since *true diversity* is considered an affirmation of the Divine. The contributors to this book, raised in different world continents, representing different genders, cultures and generations, begin to reflect this diversity. What unites these peoples is a central narrative – an outlook and framework that permeates and colours all aspects of their being. The faith that Muslims profess is simple, yet is one that has given birth to a history that is as rich and complex as any. A failure to recognise this narrative makes it difficult for one to understand the Muslim, since even the rejection of religion in such peoples must be understood from within their cultural milieu.

Caring for Muslim Patients begins with a discussion on the pattern and process of contemporary Muslim migration to Britain, information that is essential to understanding the current demography of this community (Chapter 1). Through highlighting the difficulties posed by deprivation, racial and religious discrimination, Anwar identifies important barriers that need to be overcome to promote the social, economic, and political integration of Muslims and the Muslim way of life. Winter (Chapter 2) articulates the narrative within which Muslims live and seeks to understand the continued appeal of such an all-embracing doctrine in the face of the otherwise almost relentless march of secularism. The first section of this work concludes with

Ahmed reflecting on notions of health and ill health from within traditional Muslim culture, and in particular on the intricate relationship between faith and health (Chapter 3).

Section 2 focuses on issues of direct relevance to patient care. It discusses an array of subjects ranging from challenges to the contemporary Muslim family (Chapter 4), to birth and death customs (Chapters 5 and 8), and to those dealing with periods of particular significance in the Muslim calendar such as the times of fasting (Chapter 6) and pilgrimage (Chapter 7). Peppered with anecdote and clinical cases, representing but a small proportion of the tales and experiences that now form part of our travelogues, contributors have above all aimed to provide insight – an *insider's feel* – in the belief that understanding is perhaps the key ingredient for empathy. Our conclusions are presented in Chapter 9, seeking to place this work in the context of broader historical and social discussions about the rich, complex and intriguing interface between religion, health and healthcare provision. The appendices that follow are designed to provide practical assistance to those involved in the day-to-day care of Muslims, and as a resource for those interested in gaining a broader understanding of the British Muslim community.

This work in no way exhausts the subject at hand; it should be seen as introductory and exploratory. We have been at pains to avoid promoting a stereotypical 'recipe book' approach to viewing the Muslim community in Britain. Rather, we aim to provide a foundation to begin the process of experiential learning, and the cultural context and backdrop within which the very *individual* clinical encounter should be placed. It seeks to shed light on areas of positive medical practice in the hope that an awareness of such innovation will create a climate that promotes culturally competent care to flourish and gain wider professional acceptance. It discusses issues that we believe frequently to be the cause of misunderstanding and discord between healthcare providers and their Muslim patients, and approaches are suggested that are likely to lead to more culturally sensitive healthcare. Despite its limitations this work in all probability represents the most comprehensive summary of issues concerning the care of British Muslims to date.

If the work presented here can go some way towards promoting more open, inclusive and informed dialogue about the interface between faith and health, we will have begun to discharge some of our debts. These debts we owe to those patients, colleagues and friends who, often unwittingly, whether in the consulting room, in hospital corridors, at workshops, in mosques or at family gatherings, shared with us their stories and experiences, and in so doing have served as the real inspiration for this book.

Aziz Sheikh
Abdul Rashid Gatrad
February 2000

Islam and Muslims: an overview

CHAPTER ONE

Muslims in Britain: demographic and socio-economic position

Muhammad Anwar

Muslims are now an integral part of multi-racial, multi-cultural and multi-religious Western Europe. With numbers currently estimated to exceed 8 million, they form Western Europe's largest religious minority group. A significant number have migrated to Britain in the last 50 years; their presence in this country, however, is not new.[1] The first mosque, for example, was established in Woking in 1890. In this chapter I describe the pattern and process of migration, outline demographic characteristics, and examine the social, economic and political position of the British Muslim community. Discussions on the well-established association between poverty and ill health fall beyond the scope of this chapter and will therefore not be considered. Interested readers are referred to the reports of the two independent inquiries on health inequalities commissioned by recent Conservative and Labour governments.[2,3]

Migration and the myth of return

The large-scale Muslim migration to Britain followed the conclusion of the Second World War. This process is perhaps best characterised in terms of the 'pull' factors which attracted Muslims to Britain, and the 'push' factors which forced them to leave their countries of origin.[4] The 'pull' factors included a combination of economic and social developments in Britain, and other Western European countries, during the early post-war years. A period of rapid and continuous economic growth resulted in new and upward employment opportunities for indigenous workers, particularly for those with strong educational backgrounds and specialist non-manual skills. Consequently, few indigenous workers were willing to do unskilled manual jobs or shift work, creating a labour shortage in these areas. 'Push' factors included high unemployment rates, underdevelopment and few economic opportunities in the Indian subcontinent, from where the majority of Muslim migrants trace their origins. For those migrating from countries of the New Commonwealth there were no restrictions to enter Britain until 1962, thereby allowing mass migration.

The primary migration into Britain from these regions has now almost stopped and only the reunification of families (i.e. the entry of dependants) is allowed, although this too has been made very difficult.[5] What was intended as a temporary sojourn in the West has, for many reasons, resulted in a more permanent settlement, yielding an entire generation living with the myth of return.[4]

Demographic characteristics

The size of the British Muslim community

Most Muslims have either acquired British nationality or were born in Britain. They should therefore no longer be considered as 'immigrants' but rather as 'settlers'; the same cannot be said of Muslims in some other countries of Western Europe. The largest number (about 600 000) originates from Pakistan, with sizeable groups from Bangladesh, India, Cyprus, Malaysia, Arab countries and some parts of Africa. In addition, there is a small but growing number of European Muslims.

The census is the most comprehensive source of demographic, geographical, social and economic information about the general population and ethnic minorities in Britain. Questions about ethnicity were first included in the 1991 Census, revealing an ethnic minority population that is just over 6% of the total British population. Ethnic respondents were asked to classify themselves into one of nine categories (Table 1.1).

Table 1.1:   Ethnic groupings used in the 1991 Census

- White
- Black Caribbean
- Black African
- Black other (please describe)
- Indian
- Pakistani
- Bangladeshi
- Chinese
- Any other ethnic group (please describe)

No statistics are collected through the census on religious affiliation, therefore it is difficult to estimate accurately the size of the British Muslim community. During the field trials for a possible ethnic question in the 1991 Census, a question on religious affiliations was tested with the South Asian samples. This question provided valid and reliable data and was acceptable to respondents.[6] It was not, however, included in the census test of April 1989 – a decision based on a combination of practical considerations and a lack of political will by the then Conservative government. Despite the current difficulty, I have attempted to estimate the number of Muslims in Britain using existing information sources, and present their principal demographic characteristics; summarised below are my methods. A more accurate picture should emerge following the next census in 2001 as the government has now proposed a question enquiring about religious affiliation.[7]

The most reliable method is to use data from the ethnic question in the 1991 Census coupled with information on the country of birth for those migrating from Muslim countries. However, we know that there are a significant number of Muslims that come from non-Muslim countries such as India, and there are also some Muslims, Turkish Cypriots for example, who are likely to categorise themselves as 'White'. The 'Chinese', 'Black Caribbean', 'Black African' and 'Any other ethnic group' are likely to include some Muslims, although the proportions of Muslims in these categories is difficult to estimate.

The ethnic question includes two categories, 'Pakistani' and 'Bangladeshi', representing countries with populations that are almost entirely Muslim. Table 1.2 shows the size of these two communities based on 1991 Census data.

Table 1.2:   Pakistanis and Bangladeshis in Britain (thousands), 1991

Country of origin	Britain	England	Wales	Scotland
Pakistani	477	450	6	21
Bangladeshi	163	158	4	1
Total	640	608	10	22
Total population	54 860	47 026	2835	4999

Source: 1991 Census (OPCS)

The next grouping consists of those born in Muslim countries other than Pakistan and Bangladesh, and their children. This information is available, in part, from the 'Country of birth' tables of the 1991 Census. However, no information is provided about children born to this group and numbers must therefore be estimated; the premises underlying my estimates are detailed elsewhere.[8] Two other significant communities need to be considered: those originating from India and Cyprus. These numbers again need to be estimated, using a different technique, the details of which are beyond the scope of this chapter.[8] A summary of the findings of this analysis is presented in Table 1.3.

Table 1.3:   Muslim population of Britain (thousands), 1991

Country/region of origin	Numbers
Pakistani/Bangladeshi/Indian	774
Other Asians	80
'Other other'	29
Turkish Cypriots	45
Other Muslim countries	367
African Muslims (New Commonwealth)	115
Total	1410

The figure of 1.4 million (Table 1.3) does not, however, include Muslims that come from other Muslim and non-Muslim countries of Southeast Asia such as Indonesia, the Philippines, Singapore, the Caribbean and Mauritius, to mention but a few. No 'White' Muslims are included in these calculations. Some groups of refugees, such as Kurds (Turks and Iraqis), Somalis, Bosnian and Kosovan Muslims, and the dependants of Muslims already settled here, particularly from New Commonwealth countries, who have arrived since the 1991 Census, are also not included. A conservative estimate of the number of 'White' Muslims in Britain is about 10 000. This means that several tens of thousands more Muslims could be added to the figure of 1.4 million, giving a current estimate of approximately 1.6 million.

Care must be taken, however, to minimise the risks of overestimating numbers. We know that some non-Muslims may have been included in each of the categories used in Table 1.3. For example, it is well known that there is a small Christian community in Pakistan; the same is in all probability true of the countries included in the 'Other Muslim countries' category. In reality, these numbers are very small and are, therefore, unlikely to make a significant impact on the estimated figure of 1.6 million. Extrapolating from this data, it is estimated that numbers will reach almost 2 million by 2010.

Gender

The migration of Muslims was initially predominantly male. Studying the changing male to female ratio for Pakistanis, the largest subgroup of Muslims, vividly depicts the changing structure of the British Muslim community. In 1961 for example, 82% of Pakistanis were males, while in 1982 this had dropped to only 58%. After gaining economic security, the male migrants arranged for their families to be reunified. With the continued migration of dependants from Pakistan, Bangladesh and other Muslim countries, the sex ratio is moving towards that of the indigenous White community (Table 1.4).

Table 1.4: Males per thousand females for Pakistanis, Bangladeshis, all ethnic minorities and Whites, 1991

Ethnic group	Males per 1000 females
Pakistani	1063
Bangladeshi	1160
All ethnic minorities	1001
White	935

Age profile

The Muslim population in Britain is much younger on average than the White population. There are far fewer elderly Muslims – less than 2% of Muslims aged over 65 compared with almost 17% of Whites. The picture is very different at the other end of the age spectrum, however, as almost 60% of Muslims are aged under 25 compared with 32% of Whites. Of note is that almost 60% of the British Muslim community are British born.

Household size

It is clear from Table 1.5 that Pakistani and Bangladeshi households are, on average, more than double the size of White households. Muslim households are also significantly larger than those of other ethnic minority groups. Possible explanations for this finding include the strong religious ethic encouraging fecundity and the extended nature of the Muslim family.[9]

Table 1.5: Comparison of household size (thousands) of Pakistanis and Bangladeshis with other ethnic groups, 1991

Ethnic group	Households	Household size	Households with one adult
Pakistani	101	4.81	13
Bangladeshis	31	5.34	10
Indian	226	3.80	12.9
Ethnic minorities	871	3.34	28.2
White	21 027	2.43	31.1
Entire population	21 897	2.47	31

Geographical distribution

Like other post-war migrants, Muslims settled in industrial areas where employment opportunities were most promising. Active kinship, friendship networks, and the process of chain migration, have contributed to Muslims concentrating in particular regions and cities. Country-of-birth data from the 1991 Census show that about 60% of the total British Muslim community reside in the Southeast, mainly in the Greater London area. Large communities are also found in the Midlands, West Yorkshire and the South Lancashire conurbation. Birmingham, for example, has over 100 000 Muslims, while Bradford's Muslim population is estimated to be over 60 000.

Socio-economic position

Employment

Most first-generation Muslim males were economic migrants to Britain. Consequently, their position in the labour market has, and continues to, determine their social standing both within their immediate family and in the wider community.

Muslims were granted access to a limited range of occupations – mainly unskilled or semi-skilled manual – on arrival in Britain. The demise of the industrial sector, coupled with the difficulties in finding alternative employment, led many to start their own businesses. The 1991 Census showed that 24% of all employed Pakistanis and 19% of all employed Bangladeshis had their own businesses, compared with 13% of Whites. Of these, almost 40% of Pakistanis and over 70% of Bangladeshis were employers, making an additional valuable contribution to the economy through the creation of new employment opportunities. The emergence of a second-generation British Muslim community, more versatile and better adapted to British institutions, has resulted in some diversification of employment patterns, a trend that is likely to continue.

With respect to female employment, it is interesting to note that a much lower proportion of Muslim women are in employment when compared with White women. The 1991 Census shows the economic activity rate for Pakistani and Bangladeshi women to be low, 29% and 22% respectively, compared with 71% for White women, for example.

These differences can largely be explained by religious teaching (Chapter 5), but may in addition reflect employment disadvantages faced by Muslims and other minority groups in general, and women in particular.

Evidence from the 1991 Census and Labour Force Surveys clearly shows that the unemployment rate for Muslim groups is almost three times as high as the rate for Whites (Table 1.6). There is little doubt that racial discrimination against Muslims, and other minority groups, contributes to their high levels of unemployment. Of particular concern, is that British-born and educated Muslims appear to face the same disadvantages as did the first generation of Muslim migrants. For example, in 1991 the unemployment rate for 16–24-year-old Pakistanis was almost 36%, while for White young people it was under 15%. A growing body of research indicates that this disadvantage is not confined to the lower-skilled jobs, but is also experienced when competing for well-respected professional vocations such as medicine and teaching,[10] indicating that discrimination is endemic within British society.

Table 1.6:   Unemployment rates (%) among Pakistanis, Bangladeshis and Whites, 1991

Ethnic group	Unemployment	Males	Females
Pakistani	28.8	28.5	29.6
Bangladeshi	31.7	30.9	34.5
White	8.8	8.8	6.3

Housing

I have argued elsewhere that discrimination in employment has a magnifying effect on other important areas such as education and housing.[11] The location and quality of housing may in turn impact on the quality of education and overall health status. The 1991 Census shows that Pakistanis have a high owner-occupation rate (77%) when compared with Bangladeshis (44.5%). Overall, 67% of Whites are owner-occupiers. In view of the low owner-occupation rate among Bangladeshis it is not surprising that a higher proportion of households are renting from the public sector when compared with Pakistanis (37% vs 10%). One reason for this large difference is the high concentration of Bangladeshis in inner London, particularly in Tower Hamlets, where house prices are prohibitively expensive.

The 1991 Census provides very detailed information regarding living conditions, such as overcrowding, the proportion of households with central heating, WCs and bathing facilities, and whether the accommodation is self-contained. This information shows that Muslims are quite clearly disadvantaged *vis-à-vis* their White neighbours. A large proportion of Muslim households are overcrowded (43% Pakistani and Bangladeshi), compared with only 2% of White households. Almost 60% of Pakistani and Bangladeshi households are without central heating, compared with only 37% of White households. It is also important to note that the overwhelming majority of Muslims live in inner-city, run-down areas, with the associated problems of poor amenities, high levels of crime and healthcare provision of a poorer standard further contributing to their social disadvantage.

Education

Educational issues characteristically excite passionate discussion and debate within the Muslim community, largely on account of the prevalent belief that education offers perhaps the only avenue out of poverty. Research shows that Muslims fare worse in educational achievement than do White children. For example, a recent survey has shown that Muslim children achieved lower GCSE examination results than did White children.[12] Geographical variations were noted, with Muslim children in Glasgow and some areas of London performing better on average than those in Birmingham and Bradford. Detailed analysis shows that these differences are attributable to social class and the duration of residence in Britain.

It is encouraging to see that an increasing number of Muslims are opting to pursue higher educational opportunities, despite the many biases operating against them. I have shown that there is a marked difference in acceptance rates to British universities between Muslims (40%) and Whites (54%) with identical qualifications.[13] Other education issues considered to be important by Muslims include mother-tongue teaching, religious education, provision of Halal (lawful) meals, prayer facilities, single-sex education and state funding of Muslim schools. To help place the latter issue in its correct context it is worth mentioning that although there are over 60 Muslim independent schools in Britain, only two of these have received state funding. In each of these cases this decision followed a long, and at times bitter, campaign involving Muslims the length and breadth of Britain. In contrast, there are several thousand Church of England, Catholic and Jewish schools that have voluntary-aided status and are in receipt of state funding.

Community facilities and political participation

Muslims in Britain have responded well to meet the religious and cultural needs of their communities. An extensive network of community facilities now exists, ranging from mosques to youth and women's groups. In order to organise these facilities several local and regional organisations have been formed. Current estimates are that there are over 1200 local Muslim organisations and almost 1000 mosques. Many of these mosques are in makeshift premises, usually converted houses or factories, offering only the most basic facilities. The newer mosques located within the major British cities, however, tend to be purpose-built incorporating community halls and recreational facilities for young people. There are 58 mosques in Birmingham and nearly 50 mosques in Bradford, these figures giving some insight into the importance with which British Muslims view communal prayer facilities.

A more recent development has been the emergence of national co-ordinating agencies. The Union of Muslim Organisations in the United Kingdom and Eire (UMO) is one such organisation that operates primarily through lobbying central government on issues considered to be of importance to Muslims. The Muslim Council of Britain (MCB) was launched in November 1997 as a national umbrella group; it has a current membership of over 250 Muslim organisations. Other important organisations, albeit with a more limited remit, include the United Kingdom Islamic Mission, the Islamic Foundation, the Muslim Education Trust, the National Muslim Education Council of the UK and the Council of Mosques (for contact details *see* Appendix 2).

Mosques play an important educational role in teaching children the basic tenets of Islamic faith as well as ensuring communal prayer facilities. Muslim organisations locally, regionally and now nationally, provide an opportunity for the development of religious and cultural awareness strengthening community ties. The same is true, to varying degrees, for Muslims in other Western European countries, depending on the social and legal constraints imposed by their respective governments.

Most Muslims in Britain are entitled to vote and stand for elections both as British and/or as Commonwealth citizens. The willingness of Muslims to engage in the political process is increasing, but progress in translating this willingness into significant achievements has been slow. At a local level, there are now about 150 Muslim councillors. In the recent European Parliament elections, one Muslim was elected MEP to represent the British Conservative Party. The first Muslim MP, Mohammed Sarwar, was elected in the 1997 general election representing the Labour Party for the constituency of Glasgow Govan. There need to be at least 20 Muslim MPs to reflect accurately the size of the British Muslim community. Three Muslims have recently been appointed as life peers in the House of Lords to represent the Labour Party, but again this figure needs to increase quite markedly. The representation of Muslims on public bodies is also very small. They are also under-represented in the civil service, the armed forces, the police, and judicial and other key appointments. Considering medicine, for example, it is regrettable to note that there has never been a Muslim dean of a medical school or a Muslim president of one of the Royal Colleges.

Insecurity and identity

The recent report by the Runnymede Trust Commission on *British Muslims and Islamophobia*[13] concluded that Muslims in Britain face religious discrimination and prejudice on an almost day-to-day basis, contributing significantly to the insecurity complained of by many. Among other things, the report draws attention to the stereotypical way in which Muslims are portrayed in the popular media as either 'terrorists' or 'fundamentalists', and the vulnerability of Muslims to physical violence and harassment. Muslims residing in many other Western European countries, such as France and Germany, also experience this phenomenon. The Rushdie affair, the Gulf War and more recently the genocide of Muslims in Bosnia have further contributed to this sense of vulnerability and alienation lamented on frequently by Muslims throughout Europe.

The children of first-wave Muslim migrants represent a generation caught between two cultures. They live in the culture of their parents at home but are often taught a different set of values and norms in schools, at work and through the media. Their world is not the 'old' or the 'new', but rather 'both'.[12] The process of acculturation, more marked in the youth, inevitably results in dissonance and disagreement at times between parents and their children. Thus, while the typical response of first-generation Muslims to racial taunts, or physical violence, would be an acceptance of the situation, the same cannot be said of their children. On the contrary, they can at times be heard chastising their parents on account of their passivity, arguing that a failure to respond has allowed such wrongs to continue. It is my belief that the second-generation Muslims present the real test as to how far Islamic beliefs and practices will be sustained in a non-Islamic environment, raising questions surrounding the future identity of British Muslims. My research suggests that the commitment to Islamic ethic and Muslim culture among this second generation of Muslims remains strong, though not always in the exact patterns of their parents.[12]

Summary

- Muslims form Britain's largest religious minority group. Numbers are currently estimated at around 1.6 million with a projected rise to 2 million by 2010.
- Their demography differs quite markedly to that of the indigenous White population, reflecting the process and pattern of migration to Britain. The British Muslim community has a high proportion of males and young people, and a very low proportion of elderly people.
- Racial discrimination and religious discrimination (Islamophobia) are major concerns to this community. Legislation outlawing racial discrimination has existed for over 30 years, yet despite this, racism continues to blight the day-to-day life of minority groups. Religious discrimination is still not unlawful in Britain.
- Community facilities are well developed, typically having a strong religious dimension. There is an extensive network of mosques and community groups that continue to play a central role in the life of these communities.
- Second-generation Muslims form the test case to determine the degree to which Muslims will sustain Islamic beliefs and practices in a secular environment. Initial impressions suggest that their commitment to Islam remains strong.

References and notes

1   Matter N (1998) *Islam in Britain 1558–1685.* Cambridge University Press, Cambridge.

2   Black D, Morris J, Smith C, Townsend P (1980) *Inequalities in Health: report of a research working group.* DHSS, London.

3   Acheson D, Barker D, Chambers J, Graham H, Marmot M, Whitehead M (1998) *Independent Inquiry into Inequalities in Health Report.* The Stationery Office, London.

4   Anwar M (1979) *The Myth of Return.* Heinemann, London.

5   Commission for Racial Equality (1985) *Immigration Control Procedures.* CRE, London.

6   Sillitoe K (1987) *Developing Questions on Ethnicity and Related Topics for the Census.* OPCS, London.

7   See: *The 2001 Census of Population.* White Paper presented to Parliament in March 1999 (Cm 4253).

8   Anwar M (1993) *Muslims in Britain: 1991 Census and other statistical sources.* Centre for the Study of Islam and Christian-Muslim Relations, Birmingham.

9   Anwar M (1996) *British Pakistanis.* Pakistan Forum and Birmingham City Council, Birmingham.

10 Anwar M, Ali A (1987) *Overseas Doctors: experience and expectations.* CRE, London.

11 Anwar M (1991) *Race Relations Policies in Britain: agenda for the 1990s.* Centre for Research in Ethnic Relations, Coventry.

12 Anwar M (1998) *Between Cultures.* Routledge, London.

13 Runnymede Trust (1997) *Islamophobia: a challenge for us all.* Runnymede Trust, London.

CHAPTER TWO

The Muslim grand narrative

Tim J Winter

Islam: a near neighbour

Although Islam has often served as Europe's quintessential 'Other', it is in reality a close sister religion to the Judaism and Christianity which have historically shaped the culture of the West. It shares with them a Middle Eastern origin, and a medieval experience of processes of theological articulation that took place within the context of a shared Greek patrimony. Muslim theology, no less than the religious thought of medieval Christian and Jewish intellectuals such as Aquinas and Maimonides, is a complex and brilliant fusion of the Semitic and the Hellenic spirit: Plato and Moses are the property of Muslims no less than of Christians and Jews. Moreover Islam is the only non-Christian religion to accord specific recognition to Jesus, the central figure in traditional Western European religion, whom Muslims revere as a healer, a perfect messenger of God (Allah) and as a miracle-working Messiah, although, like Unitarians, Muslims do not accept the doctrine of his divinity.

Despite a superficial strangeness, Islam must hence be classed as a thoroughly Western religion. Its inclusion of Jesus of Nazareth provides one sign of this; but a still more significant connection is supplied by the figure of Abraham. This 'knight of faith' serves for Muslims, as he has for Christians such as Kierkegaard, as the model of a primordial believer, the upholder of a simple monotheism and a pristine moral code. Muhammad, like his forefather Abraham, was cast out by his own people when he opposed their worship of idols and challenged their indifference to the poor; and Islam's holiest site, the Great Sanctuary at Mecca, recalls the Patriarch's desert exile, where Abraham built what The Qur'an describes as the first religious building on earth, the Ka'bah.

Five Pillars of faith

In this sense, the *Hajj*, one of the five cardinal obligations (Table 2.1) that support the spirituality of every observant Muslim, is a rhetorical statement of Islam's understanding of its place in sacred history. The resonances of this spectacular event are powerfully Abrahamic: the seven courses between two Meccan hillocks recall the quest of Hagar for water for the infant Ishmael, a quest which led to the miracle of the Well of Zamzam which flows to this day. After completing their sevenfold procession around the Ka'bah, the pilgrims pray where Abraham and Ishmael stood during the building of this primordially simple, cubical structure. Later, the culminating ritual takes place at the plain of Arafat, seven miles from Mecca, where the world's largest multi-ethnic gathering assembles each year to pray near the Mount of Mercy, revered as the site where the Prophet Muhammad delivered his Farewell Sermon. Standing to petition Allah, the pilgrims recall the final resurrection, when Allah, surveying the quality of human hearts, judges the quick and the dead, and decrees their future, beyond time, in heaven or in hell.

Table 2.1: The Five Pillars of faith

• *Shahadah*	The testimony of faith
• *Salah*	The five daily ritual prayers
• *Zakat*	Annual obligatory alms tax for the poor
• *Sawm*	Fasting during the month of *Ramadan*
• *Hajj*	The annual pilgrimage to Mecca

The *Hajj* is thus simultaneously the sign of what is familiar and unfamiliar about Islam: it claims Abrahamic ancestry, but with an Ishmaelite voice. Judaism and hence Christianity trace their Abrahamic descent through Isaac, while Islam follows a different covenantal tradition represented in the person of his elder brother Ishmael. The Ishmaelites are marginal to the Biblical tradition, but Islam reveres Ishmael as a prophet, whose half-Gentile blood anticipates the destiny of the Ishmaelite covenant to encompass the entire world. Hence Islam's traditional self-image as the only divinely purposed universal religion, and as the dispensation designed to bring Abraham to the world. Mirroring this theological hope, the medieval Islamic community stretched across a vast territory from the Pyrenees to Bengal and beyond; and, while recognisably Abrahamic in its beliefs and worship, acknowledged the specific genius of each of its constituent peoples, who in most cases were not Arabised, but developed their own cultural expressions of the faith, allowing vibrant religious literatures to develop in Persian, Turkish, Hausa, Malay and the hundreds of other vernaculars of the Muslim world. Architecture, from the Great Mosque of Cordova, through the Blue Mosque of Istanbul, to the faience splendours of Isfahan, and still further east, the Taj Mahal, displays this recurrent theme of unity in diversity, of a religious tradition able to accommodate and fertilise and enrich, rather than reduce, the cultures which owe it allegiance. The fact that the Muslim Abraham is seen from so many different angles gives the lie to all stereotypes of Islam as a religious monolith.

The rich diversity of historic Islam, which the *Hajj* symbolises, was further facilitated by the tradition's reluctance to support a hierarchy. Islam has never been, in the conventional sense, 'organised religion'. Its insistence on direct human dealing with a God whose generosity guarantees a gracious response to the prayers and penitence of his creatures eliminates any need for sacraments, or for a hierarchy of priests and bishops to administer them. The only authorities are the '*ulema*', literally the 'learned', men (and sometimes women) trained in traditional schools to a level at which they can dispense guidance to others. But these experts possess no automatic authority, and again we find that classical Islam has here embraced an often-bewildering diversity, recognising several distinct theological orientations and at least four canonical traditions of law and worship. Often perceived in the West as univocal, Islamic theology and law have always in reality been richly diverse, and on the many issues which have not been definitively and unambiguously set down in the Muslim scriptures, are showing themselves no less subject to revision in our time than in the past. Issues such as abortion, contraception, genetic engineering, women's roles and many others trigger lively debates among Muslims, disclosing today as never before the absence of an Islamic 'orthodoxy'. Without a church hierarchy to define normality, the tradition slowly evolves by consensus, through discussion of current needs in the light of the scriptures. An absolute uniformity of opinions almost never ensues.

The lack of a hierarchy is evident in another of Islam's 'Five Pillars', the daily worship known as *Salah* (in the Arab world and Africa) and as *Namaz* in Turkey, Iran and the Indian subcontinent. This practice is obligatory upon all men and women, if they are sane and adult (adulthood denoting sexual maturity in boys and menarche in girls). Just as the physically frail are excused the *Hajj*, so too those who cannot perform the full movements of the *Salah*, which, in line with Islam's positive view of the body, entails an interaction of physical and spiritual activity, are required to do only what they can accomplish without risk of exacerbating their condition. The healthy must pray in a clean place, usually on a prayer-carpet, facing the Ka'bah (in England, about 120°, or east-southeast), as they recite the Qur'an in Arabic and follow a series of movements which include positions of standing, bowing and prostration. The times appointed for this brief but dignified rite are as follows: *Fajr* (between first light and dawn), *Zuhr* (noon until mid-afternoon), *Asr* (mid-afternoon until sunset), *Maghrib* (just after sunset) and *Isha* (when the sky is completely dark, until midnight, or until the time for *Fajr*).

For those who are able, the *Salah* must be preceded by brief, ritual ablutions known as *wudu* (in Turkish, *abtest*), which entail the washing with clean water of the mouth, nostrils, face, hands and forearms, the wiping of the head and ears, and the washing of the feet. Those too ill to do this carry out the ritual of *tayammum* instead, which simply involves touching a stone or clean dust with both hands, and moving the hands over the face, hands and forearms.[1]

In the lavatory, the practice of *istinja* requires the use of running water to wash the genitals and anus after urination or evacuation. Without this, the *Salah* is not regarded as valid, unless, again, the practice would entail difficulty or danger for a patient. The Prophet Muhammad insisted that those entitled to be excused any such duty carried no blame, and he would grow angry with sick people who, out of misplaced piety, performed ablution rites which might endanger their health.

A further ritual purity practice is *ghusl*. This entails passing clean running water over the entire body (usually today in a shower), and is required after sexual intercourse or ejaculation, and, for women, every month after menstruation has ceased.[2]

The five daily prayers are preferably said in mosques, which, depending on region and custom, may or may not have space for women. In these austere, uncluttered spaces the prayers are led by an *imam*, who may be any male member of the congregation able to recite the Qur'an correctly and to deliver a sermon before the noon congregational prayer each Friday (the *jum'a* prayer).[3] In some Muslim cultures the *imam* has pastoral responsibilities as well, and may advise on belief and practice, and counsel individuals who seek his help. But although he is a revered figure, his authority is not automatic; neither does he form part of a hierarchy, as typically he is chosen and paid by the local mosque committee, which is answerable only to the congregation. Although *imams* often undertake hospital visits, they have no sacraments to administer, and there are no formal last rites or extreme unction, with the consequence that they are never religiously indispensable. Often patients will prefer to be visited by devout and knowledgeable elders or relations, or by devout members of the local community, whose prayers are regarded as especially reliable.

The duty of *Salah*, then, while formal and often collective, does not locate the believer within a parish or in obedience to a hierarchy. The rite is believed to establish a direct, unmediated connection with the divine presence (the Arabic word *Salah* signifies 'connection'), as symbolised by the turn towards the Ka'bah, and to bring a sense of ease and of burdens lifted. In a parable, the Prophet taught that to pray with sincerity five times in every day resembles washing with the same frequency from a stream running outside one's house. Delayed prayers can lead to anxiety and guilt; prayers performed in serenity trigger a contemplative and relaxed state of mind, a sense of peaceful submission to the will and good providence of Allah, and a state of harmony with the created world, every creature in which, according to the Qur'an, is also adoring Allah in its own way.[4]

The *Salah* links the religious life of the believer to the rolling of the planet beneath his or her feet; while the movements of the moon govern the time of the Hajj. The Islamic calendar contains 12 lunar months, with the result that Islamic dates fall some ten days earlier in each year of the Western calendar. All the festivals hence migrate forward in this way; one of the most conspicuous being *Eid ul-Adha*, which commemorates the end of the *Hajj*. Another festival is *Eid ul-Fitr*, which ends the fasting month of *Ramadan*.[5]

Although optional fasts are often observed at other times of the year, *Ramadan* itself is considered one of the Five Pillars of the religion. This key rite, which requires adult, sane and healthy Muslims to abstain from food, drink, tobacco and sexual relations from first light until sunset, forms the subject of a separate chapter in this book (Chapter 7). Religiously it is understood as a means of detaching oneself from worldly, material cravings, thus allowing the spiritual seeker to focus on Allah without distraction. On the moral plane, it is believed to help the rich to empathise with the sufferings of the hungry.

A further technique for achieving spiritual detachment is the practice of *Zakat*. This Arabic word means both 'purification' and 'growth', and refers specifically to the duty to donate one fortieth of one's wealth in charity each year. In the Muslim understanding, wealth is a loan from Allah, and is to be gratefully celebrated by allocating alms for the poor, thereby 'purifying' the remainder and bringing spiritual growth through the practice of renunciation. In addition to the 'Pillar' which is the *Zakat*, the Prophet encouraged his followers to practice alms-giving of a less formal kind, which in Britain often takes the form of remittances to needy relations in countries of origin, or of donations to the numerous Muslim charities or to mosques.

The practices of *Salah*, *Hajj*, *Zakat* and the *Ramadan* fast are simultaneously the expression and strengthening of the core of Muslim theology, which is like a thumb to its four fingers. This is articulated by the *Shahada*, the 'Testimony of Faith', which runs 'There is no deity but Allah; and Muhammad is Allah's messenger'. This simple creed locates the believer within a world of meaning and identity, the divinely gifted response to which is affirmed in the forms of worship, fasting, pilgrimage and charity. It is constantly on the lips of the devout: whispered into the ear of a newborn infant or a dying parent, it frames and defines the believer's experience.

In this way, the Five Pillars of Islam lay down the warp and woof of the Muslim life. The *Shahada* is intended to be a constant presence; the day is punctuated by the five prayers, and the week by the Friday congregational prayer, while the *Zakat* and the *Ramadan* fast occur once a year, with the *Hajj* coming once in a lifetime. Linking the believer to the movements of the earth, the sun and the moon, these ancient monotheistic rites, practised without alteration since the time of the Prophet, are believed to work a spiritual alchemy on the soul of the Muslim by providing a constant reminder of the beauty and truth which underlie and give meaning to the visible world.

The human condition

The connection with nature, which forms so fundamental a theme of the religion, has a theological basis rooted in the Muslim understanding of the human condition. The Qur'anic account of the Fall differs from the Biblical version in allowing Adam a full repentance, thus wiping out the stain of original sin.[6] In Muslim teaching, children are born without sin, so that tendencies to selfishness and vice result from nurture, rather than nature. Heaven and not Hell is the natural destination of humanity even after the Fall; and this belief in Allah's generosity is strengthened further by the Prophet's teaching that a good deed is rewarded tenfold. Good intentions, even if not put into practice, are still rewarded by Allah, while bad intentions are not punished if they are never actualised.

Human intelligence is valorised, and the Prophet's dictum that 'the noblest thing Allah has created is the intellect'[7] lies at the root of the Islamic prohibition of alcohol and other narcotics. Because the body is affirmed as a positive creation of Allah, extreme forms of asceticism and mortification are alien to Muslim piety, as are tattooing and some forms of cosmetic surgery.[8] Sexuality is valued, and the Muslim scriptures confirm that the sex act with one's spouse brings a rich reward from Allah, while celibacy is frowned upon. However, Islam maintains strict standards of sexual morality, forbidding sexual relations with any person to whom one is not married. The seclusion of a man and woman together is regarded as a sign of low standards, as is the unnecessary exposure of the body. Hence women and men are encouraged to dress in a dignified way that often seems at odds with Western norms.[9] In particular, women traditionally cover their bodies when outside their family context, showing only the face, hands and feet. Such traditions, indifference to which can cause considerable embarrassment and discomfort, reflect not only the religion's understanding of public morality and decency, but also its theological valorising of the human body, seen as a manifestation of the sacred which must be unveiled only in the most reverent and private context.[10,11]

Islam's view of humanity may thus be described as upbeat. The Prophet himself 'loved optimism', we are told, and, in the tradition's memory, 'smiled more than any other man'. Without a doctrine of original sin, and with an affirmative attitude to the mind and the body, Muslim cultures have historically favoured a relaxed and genial lifestyle. Medieval castles in England were draughty and austere affairs, while contemporary Muslim palaces, of which the Alhambra in Granada is only the best-known example, were dedicated to the arts of refined and comfortable living. The fall of the Roman Empire prompted the closure of the public baths across Europe; the rise of Islam elevated the public bath (the *ham*) into a major social institution. Even today, in countries from Morocco to Turkey to the subcontinent, complex massage and grooming practices in the often-splendid surroundings of the *hammam* indicate one way in which Muslims enjoy a religious ethos that combines both hygiene and relaxation.

The way of Muhammad

The spectacular diversity of Muslim cultures has as one point of unity the figure of Abraham; but the practical model and exemplar is always his Ishmaelite descendent, Muhammad.[12] The Prophet of Islam died in the year 632, but as the millions who annually visit his tomb in Madina demonstrate, he remains the role model for Islamic piety and holiness. The Prophet was, quite possibly, the most influential man in history,[13] and although he remains insufficiently known in the West, for Muslims he is revered as a constant inspirational presence. While any idea of his divinity is vigorously resisted, as he called himself 'nothing but Allah's slave', veneration of the Prophet is central to the piety of traditional Muslim cultures and supplies one of the key spiritual energies of the religion.[14] The Biblical prohibition on graven images is maintained in Islam, but litanies and poetry, typically of a joyful temper, exist in every Muslim language to describe and sing the Prophet's praises. He is viewed as a hero who suffered persecution and violence from his Meccan contemporaries, and who then, following his migration to Madina in 622, adopted a 'liberation theology' which challenged the tribal structures of Arabia in order to establish a model state in which tribal differences were abolished. Popular themes in devotional literature about the Prophet include his poverty: he lived in a windowless house with a piece of sackcloth for a door and refused to sleep at night until he had given to the poor any food or money which remained in his house. Other themes are his habit of visiting the sick (a particularly meritorious practice in Islam, as those with experience of overcrowded Muslim bedsides will know), his lack of affectation (he often walked barefoot or bareheaded, he swept his house and patched his own clothes), his refusal ever to accept *Zakat* money for himself, and his patience with the often overbearing and crude desert nomads. The reception of the Qur'an, which, as Allah's literal speech conveyed by the Angel Gabriel is regarded as a text so holy that many Muslims will not permit outsiders even to touch it, is considered one of his supreme merits.

A medieval devotional portrait of Muhammad – Allah's final emissary

He maintained friendly and loyal ties with his relatives, but without preferring them to anyone who was superior to them. He never snubbed anyone. He accepted the excuse of anyone who made an excuse. He would joke, but would never say anything that was not true. He would laugh, but not uproariously. He would watch permissible games and sports, and would not criticise them. He ran races with his wives. Voices would be raised around him, and he would be patient. He kept a sheep, from which he would draw milk for his family. He would walk among the fields of his companions. He never despised any pauper for his poverty or illness; neither did he hold any king in awe simply because he was a king. He would call rich and poor to Allah, without distinction.

Abu Hamid al-Ghazali[15]

Love for the Prophet is hence central in the Muslim affective range. Allah is held in awe and respect; the Prophet is loved. Thus committed Muslims never utter or hear his name without repeating the words, 'Allah bless him and send him peace!' (*salla'Llahu alayhi wa-sallam*). This love in turn informs and energises a cardinal duty of the faith, which is the faithful emulation of the Prophet's *Sunnah*: his custom, or way of life.

The Muslim *imitatio* of the Prophet can appear odd to outsiders, and only becomes coherent in the light of the emotion of love and reverence in which the 'Best of Creation' is held. Pious Muslims regard his human and spiritual perfection as a model to be emulated in all circumstances. He ate sitting on a rug on the floor, using his right hand, after invoking Allah; and many traditional Muslims do likewise. The interior of a fully traditional Muslim home recalls the simplicity of the Prophet's life: the absence of furniture is believed to engender an atmosphere of uncluttered serenity. To sit on the floor, Muslims believe, in the mosque or at home, serves to reduce the emotional distance between fellow human beings.

Love for the Prophet also animates more formal aspects of Muslim tradition such as dietary rules. Pork is forbidden, as is the flesh of animals or birds whose lives have been taken by idolaters or atheists. Fish is permissible, as is lamb, beef or chicken slaughtered by Muslims in a way which is *halal* (permissible). Most Muslims will eat kosher meat, as this is prepared in a similar way and has been slaughtered by believers in God; many Muslims will also eat meat killed by Christians.

Again following the Prophet's example, there are traditions of effusive greeting involving handshaking and embraces, accompanied by the phrase *Assalamu-Alaikum*: 'Peace be upon you'.

The *Sunnah* is applicable to both sexes, with important differentiation, and although the debate over women's rights and roles is sharp in modern Islam, with believers defending a wide spectrum of opinions, Muslims are anxious to point to the evidence for Islam's high esteem for women.[16,17] Because Allah is ungendered, there is no cosmic prioritising of the male principle. The Five Pillars are incumbent upon both sexes, and salvation is open to men and women alike. In many Muslim societies the oppression of women is frequent, as it is in many other traditional cultures (such as some Christian cultures of Latin America or certain Hindu environments), but Muslims insist that such abuses are the product of un-Islamic cultural values that have survived an Islamisation process that has seldom been much more than partial. For this reason women have often been at the forefront of calls to bring to the modern Muslim world forms of Islamic government, however variously this is understood.

The major Islamic denominations recognise the decisive authority of the Prophet's *Sunnah*. Ninety percent of the world's Muslims (and an even higher percentage in the United Kingdom) are *Sunnis*, who subscribe to the version of Islam outlined in this chapter. The great majority of the remainder are *Shi'is* (collectively known as *Shi'a*), who were distinguished from the mainstream community after the Prophet's death on the basis of their conviction that his descendants alone should be the successors to his temporal authority. The practical and doctrinal differences between *Sunnis* and *Shi'is* are relatively slight, perhaps the most conspicuous being the *Shi'a* practice of combining prayers so as to pray on only three occasions in each day, and of breaking the fast at least half an hour after sunset.

Sunnis and *Shi'is* share one view and experience of Islam, which is that it represents all imaginable human compassion and dignity. Western images, fed by a mass media preoccupied with extremist minorities and indifferent to mainstream piety, are unrecognisable and often deeply offensive to traditional believers, for whom Islam is nothing less than a synonym for goodness. Stripped of cultural encrustation or associations with political extremism overseas, it is a religion which is not only easily understood, given the simplicity of its doctrine and the optimism of its world-view, but is easily respected for the standards which it introduces to the often confused moral landscape of contemporary Britain.

Summary

- Although frequently perceived as an 'outsider', Islam is in actual fact a close sister religion to Judaism and Christianity. Born of the same ancient Semitic soil, Islam regards itself as nothing other than a continuation and culmination of the pristine message of the Biblical Prophets.
- Core aspects of the Muslim faith, namely the insistence on monotheism, a regard for the sacred in all walks of life and belief in a final accountability, are very intimately linked to the Judeo-Christian narrative, which has traditionally shaped the culture of the West.
- Many of the most evident aspects of Muslim culture, such as race, dress customs, cookery and language, are functions not of the religion proper, but of the specifics of regional culture in the countries of origin. Islam continues to respect and value such diversity, so long as it does not transgress the boundaries of Sacred Law.
- The end to primary immigration of Muslims will lead to an inexorable increase in the percentage of British-born Muslims. Though these second- and third-generation Muslims are discarding aspects of regional culture, core values of the faith remain strong, thereby allowing the strong doctrinal and moral affinity between Islam and more traditional aspects of British religion and culture to become more widely recognised.
- For the majority of Muslims in Britain, Islam is nothing less than a synonym of goodness.

References and notes

1 Keller NHM (1995) *The Reliance of the Traveller*, pp 60–92. Amana, Maryland.
2 Keller NHM (1995) *The Reliance of the Traveller*, pp 93–5. Amana, Maryland.
3 Children, the sick and the frail elderly are not required to attend any mosque service.
4 Sheikh A (1997) Quiet room is needed in hospitals for prayer and reflection. *BMJ.* **315**: 1625.
5 Ahsan MM (1985) *Muslim Festivals*. Wayland, Hove.

6   Anawati MM (1958) Islam and the immaculate conception. In: D O'Connor
    (ed) *The Dogma of the Immaculate Conception*. University of Notre Dame Press,
    Notre Dame.

7   al-Munajjid SA (1987) *Al-'Aql*, p 12. Dar Nasr, Beirut.

8   Rispler-Chaim V (1993) *Islamic Medical Ethics in the Twentieth Century*.
    Brill, Leiden.

9   Naficy H (1999) Veiled visions, powerful presences. In: R Issa, R Whitaker
    (eds) *Life and Art: the new Iranian cinema*. National Film Theatre, London.

10 Bouhdhiba A (1985) *Sexuality in Islam*. Routledge, London.

11 Musallam B (1983) *Sex and Society in Islam*. Cambridge University Press,
    Cambridge.

12 Lings M (1993) *Muhammad: his life based on the earliest sources*. George Allen
    and Unwin, London.

13 If we divide the credit for the foundation of Christianity between Christ and
    St Paul, this is a readily defensible position.

14 Schimmel A (1985) *And Muhammad is His messenger: the veneration of the
    Prophet in Islamic piety*. University of North Carolina Press, Chapel Hill.

15 al-Ghazali AH (1927) *Ihya' 'Ulum al-Din* (The revival of the religious
    sciences), vol II, pp 319–20. al-Halabi, Cairo.

16 Badawi L (1994) Islam. In: J Holm, J Bowker (eds) *Women in Religion*. Pinter,
    London.

17 Murata S (1992) *The Tao of Islam: a sourcebook on gender relationships in Islamic
    thought*. State University of New York Press, Albany.

CHAPTER THREE

Health and disease: an Islamic framework

Abdul Aziz Ahmed

An individual's understanding of concepts such as 'health' and 'disease' arise from a complex interaction between personal experiences and a range of cultural factors that may include, among other things, language, family values and norms, and religion.[1] The relative importance of each of these factors in determining one's outlook may vary quite substantially between cultures, and in pluralist societies such as Britain, from one subculture to another. In those communities that retain a sense of the sacred, the influence of religion on shaping the individual and communal view is often quite considerable.[2] My experience of studying, teaching and living with disparate Muslim communities, in four different continents, suggests that this is certainly true with respect to Muslims. An appreciation of religious ethic surrounding health and disease may therefore aid professionals in the challenging role of delivering care in a manner that is appropriate and culturally sensitive.[3] This chapter delineates and explores the nature of health and ill health from within the Islamic world-view. An etymological approach is adopted, drawing on Qur'anic lexicons and Arabic commentaries on classical Islamic texts, for linguistic competence and religious understanding are regarded as inseparable within classical Muslim thought.

Health, disease and the human heart

*There is in the body a piece of flesh, and if it is good
the entire body is good.
However, if it is diseased, the entire body is diseased;
and know, it is the heart.*

Prophet Muhammad[4]

Man's essence

Man – Allah's masterpiece creation – is fundamentally different from all
other beings. The most important distinction is that he has both an
external and internal reality. His external being, his *corpus*, is that
which he shares with the rest of creation. The central point of his
inwardness, the domain of the spirit and soul, is the *qalb*, or the human
heart. The human stands distinct and indeed elevated above all else in
creation, whether in the animal or angelic realm, on account of this
inward dimension, for this is his essence – the isthmus between the
temporal and eternal worlds. Ultimately then, all humans will be judged
according to the 'health' of this inner reality, for as the Prophet
constantly reminded the men and women of faith, 'Allah does not look
to your bodies, nor your forms, but rather He looks to your hearts'.

The preceding chapter, *The Muslim grand narrative*, described how
Man's separation from the Divine, following Adam's Fall, is temporary –
his intended destiny is one of return. Born healthy, in a primordial pure
state (*al-fitra*), so long as he preserves and maintains this condition he
can be assured that his lot in the eternal life hereafter will be one of
bliss, satisfaction, and a deep and lasting peace.

Qalb, an Arabic term, refers to 'the essence and most inner aspect of
a thing', differentiating and demarcating it from all else. The *qalb* of a
palm tree for example, is the seed of its fruit. Without a seed the date
could not and would not have existed. If a tree produces no seed, it is, in
the desert Arab's view, useless, but through its seeds it is eternal. The
'healthy heart' that is mentioned in the Prophetic tradition cited above
is thus far more than a strong and efficient coronary organ.

The states of the heart

*And let me not be in disgrace on the Day when men will be
raised up; the Day when neither wealth nor sons will avail,
but only he will prosper that brings to Allah a sound heart.*

Qur'an[5]

And in their hearts is a disease.

Qur'an[6]

The verb from which the word *qalb* is derived also means 'to turn'
(*yan qalibo*). The heart can turn in many directions. In whichever
direction it turns the body will follow, for as al-Ghazali (d. 1111) – the
celebrated medieval theologian and logician – remarked of the heart, 'it
is the king who is obediently followed by the other limbs; if the king is
upright and good then his servants will be likewise'.[7]

In Arabic, one who is sound and healthy is said to be *salim*. Classical
Arabic dictionaries define *salim* as 'the one who has been stung or bitten
by a snake'.[8] In pre-Islamic Arabia, the snakebite was considered to be a
good omen; indicating future well being. With the arrival of Islam the
meaning of *salim* evolved. Muslims began to see a healthy state, or the
state of being *salim*, as one in which a person can see the will of Allah
even in times of adversity and tribulation – being bitten by a desert snake
was but one example of such an affliction.

The *salim* will therefore not see illness as punishments, but rather as
'tests' from Allah; these tests afford the opportunity to deal with many
of the ills of the heart (Table 3.1) – the diseases of material attachment
and the associated tendency to forget Allah, for example. According to
an oft-repeated tradition, sickness and tribulation bring an opportunity
to earn reward through patience and steadfastness and are a cause for
the cleansing of one's sins. The Prophet said: 'No Muslim will be
afflicted by hardship or illness, or anxiety or worry, or harm or sadness,
even the pricking of a thorn, except that, by it, Allah will cover up some
of his sins'.[9] It has been argued by some Muslim scholars that the
greater the illness, the greater is the reward. While the Prophet lay
dying with fever, one of his companions suggested that his pain and
fever was twice that of others. When he enquired whether this indicated
that he would receive a double reward, the Prophet responded in the
affirmative, adding: 'A Muslim is not afflicted with illness, or the like,
other than (through this experience) Allah sheds from him his mistakes,

just like a tree sheds its leaves'.[10] Muslim literature is rich with accounts of the companions of the Prophet, who would often worry, thinking Allah had forsaken them if they went for extended periods without being afflicted or, from their perspective, blessed through illness. This does not, however, mean that they actively sought situations where physical ailments were likely, or that they failed to seek a cure when problems occurred. On the contrary, based on the advice and encouragement of the Prophet, from the earliest times Muslims have been committed to and engaged in medicinal practice (*see below*).

Table 3.1:   The states of the heart

The healthy heart	*The diseased heart*
Belief in Allah	Disbelief in Allah
Sincerity of purpose	Hypocrisy
Humility	Arrogance
Hope in Allah's good Providence	Despairing of Allah's mercy
Contentment	Dissatisfaction
Regard for Sacred Law	Disdain for Sacred Law
Divine Love	Material and temporal love

In Semitic languages, words are generally derived from a three-lettered root term. A number of related words stem from this same root, and an appreciation of these derivatives helps in developing a fuller understanding of the concept being considered. *Salim* then is derived from the root S-L-M; other derivatives of this term include *salama* (safety), *salaam* (the Muslim greeting of peace), *Islam* (the way of peace) and *Muslim* (one who has voluntarily surrendered his will to the Divine will, and so is in a state of peace). A *qalb salim*, or healthy heart, when considered in its fullest sense, is an organ that is whole, sound, content and at peace, directing the rest of the body in the pursuit of good, where good is defined as following of Sacred Law. Since this is the path that leads back to the Ancestral Home there can be no higher good. Similar meanings can be found in other sacred cultures – healing and holiness stem from the same root term for example, both words suggesting a sense of wholeness, a theme that dominated early and medieval Christian notions of health.[11]

An Arab maxim teaches that to understand a particular notion one must understand its antithesis. If a healthy heart leads towards eternity, the diseased heart (*qalb marid*) is preoccupied with the temporal, content in self-gratification, self-indulgence and a disregard for Sacred Law. One with a diseased heart will thus neither be able to contextualise illness nor know how to conduct himself in such a situation. Despair, discontentment and dissatisfaction with Allah's plan characterises an unsound heart in such situations. Many of the psychological problems that plague today's world, stress, anxiety and depression to mention but a few, reflect the improvised condition of modern man.[12] In his arrogance he fails to recognise the very essence of being, and is as a result deprived of any inward sustenance.

Hope and fear – qualities of a sound heart

A young man lay dying at the time of the Prophet Muhammad. 'How are you?' the Prophet enquired. 'Hoping in my Lord, but fearful on account of my sins' he replied. The Prophet then declared: 'Never do these two emotions unite in the heart of a Muslim, in such a situation as this, but that Allah gives him what he hopes for, and gives him safekeeping from that which he fears'.[13]

Healing the heart

The Qur'an makes little mention of physical illness, its primary focus being attending to the state of the heart. Through a combination of encouragement, enticement, warning and exhortation it seeks to remind (*dhikr*) the human heart, an organ that is liable to frequently forget its true purpose, of the transience of the life of this world and the reward that awaits those who remain steadfast and pure. It is for this reason that the Qur'an – Allah's final revelation – chooses to describe itself as *as-Shifa*, or 'a healing', asserting categorically that 'it is only in the mention of Allah that hearts find rest'.[14]

The physical state

Allah did not send down a sickness except that He sent down its cure.

Prophet Muhammad[15]

The rights of the body

Sacred Law articulates certain rights to the body, above all being the right that it is accorded respect, whether in life or death, for by definition man is its temporary custodian. The body needs to be maintained and attended to and it is for this very reason that much of Sacred Law exists, with its insistence on matters of cleanliness and personal hygiene, wholesome food and drink (*halal*), and providing the body with the due amounts of exercise and rest. The concept of 'balance' is central to the Qur'anic message, for just as the cosmos is in balance, so must be its principal inhabitant.

The development of healthcare

'There is a cure for every malady save one – that of old age'[16] said the noble Prophet in a famous tradition, placing a personal responsibility on the one with an ailment to seek its remedy. For this, rather than use incantations or sorcery, as was common in pre-Islamic Arabia, the believers were encouraged to seek the services of one trained in the appropriate sciences, while nonetheless being aware that cure ultimately resides in the hands of *As-Shafi*, 'The Supreme Healer'.[17]

Traditionally this call has been heeded with seriousness, and it is interesting to note that one of the first sciences to flourish in the lands won over to Islam was that of medicine. Notions of an imbalance in the humours, as was the prevalent belief in Antiquity, resonated with the views of many within the early Muslim communities, acting as a catalyst for the so-called 'age of translations'. This was by anyone's accounts a remarkable episode in the history of medicine, for while much of Europe had plundered into 'The Dark Ages', Christian and Muslim scholars, under official state patronage, were busy translating, commenting on and critiquing Greek, and also Persian and Indian, medical scholarship, seeking improved understanding, and ultimately cure, for conditions for which effective remedies were lacking. Interest in medicinal practice has always been central to Muslim piety, for there are literally scores of prophetic traditions placing great esteem on helping and aiding one's fellow man in his hour of need.

With access to the learning that had accrued over centuries in many of the most important traditions of the time, Muslim scholarship quickly turned its attention to the synthesis and dissemination of this body of teaching. The towering figures of the Persian philosopher-physicians Muhammad ibn-Zakariya al-Rhazi (d. 925) and Abu Ali al-Husayn ibn Abdullah ibn Sina (d. 1037), known to the West as Rhazes and Avicenna respectively, represent the pinnacle of this synthesis phase, with their compendia dominating medical curricula in the Muslim and Christian worlds for well over five centuries. The Spanish-born Abul-Qasim al-Zahrawi (d. 1013) and Ahmad ibn Muhammad ibn Rushd (d. 1198), Latinized as Albucasis and Averroes respectively, indicate the breadth and depth of the learning and dissemination culture that the Qur'an, with its repeated emphasis on learning and teaching, fostered.[18]

Improvements in clinical care were of paramount importance, and much important advancement was made to existing practice. These included the first network of regular and mobile hospitals (*bimaristan*) seeking to offer medical care free of charge, irrespective of gender, race or religious affiliation, and the first centres devoted to the humane care of the insane (*maristan*). Considerable advancements were made in the field of medical ethics, the most notable contributions coming from the pen of one Ishaq ibn Ali al-Rahawi who, during the second half of the ninth century, laid the foundations for *Adab al-Tabib* (The Ethics of the Physician), reminding physicians that they were charged with maintaining both body and soul. Medical education and registration were other fields that benefited from Muslim contributions, with the concept of re-accreditation of physicians gaining importance for the first time in 10th-century Baghdad.[18,19]

The potted and sketchy history of Muslim contributions to medicine here presented is in no way meant to be comprehensive, but rather to reflect the importance attached to medicine from the earliest of times. The oft-repeated myth that Muslims sole contribution to medicine (and the sciences) was the preservation of Hellenistic learning owes more to the imperialistic vision that characterised post-Renaissance Europe than to any objective reading of history. This interest continues, as evidenced by the desire of many a Muslim parent that their children enter the healing profession – and in view of the Qur'anic reminder, 'That whosoever saves a human life, it is as if they have saved the whole of humankind',[20] that such sentiments are expressed should perhaps come as no great surprise.

Exporting the Qur'anic framework

Arabic – the language of the Qur'an – is the source *par excellence* through which Muslim culture traces its roots. As non-Arab nations embraced the Islamic vision, they adopted many Arabic terms for key concepts. The degree to which this occurred varied from region to region. Northwest Africa, for example, became almost completely Arabised, while other regions, such as Southeast Asia, only assimilated religious terms. The impact of Qur'anic Arabic in these latter regions should not however be underestimated because although only a few hundred terms may have been adopted, many of these have assumed positions of pivotal importance in defining important concepts in these communities. The word *afiya*, for example, which denotes a sense of wholeness and totality, is used in modern Swahili for health; similarly, *dawa*, signifying a means to achieve cure, is currently used in Urdu for medication. With the transfer of these Qur'anic terms came a shift in, or refinement of, these concepts. Perhaps most noteworthy of all is that the greeting of peace – *Assalamu-Alaikum* (a derivative of *salim*) – is in universal use among Muslims, be they in majority or minority communities. These few examples illustrate the extent to which such Qur'anic terms have permeated the language and culture of non-Arab Muslim nations.

Where worlds meet

No, no, I disagree!

'Depression is very common in the Muslim community, and our attempts at treating it effectively are hampered by the stigma attached to the diagnosis' opined a Muslim psychiatrist.

'It's not right to consider depression as a physical ailment – it reflects a lack of faith' retorted someone from the floor.

Exasperated, the psychiatrist tried again: 'You see, this is just what I mean!'

There then followed a long, and at times, heated discussion on Islamic perspectives on health and disease. After considerable discussion and debate, and with no clear conclusions drawn, the Chairman tactfully steered the discussion on to a less contentious issue.

Muslim Health Conference, London

Familiar to anthropologists is the phenomena of acculturation – the process through which a minority group will incorporate some of the cultural attributes of the larger society. Being confronted with a British tradition that has all but neglected the inner reality, and for whom the heart is considered no more than a biological pump, has for many Muslims in Britain caused considerable dissonance with the traditional view of understanding health and disease. Being caught between contrasting and at times conflicting world-views has resulted in confusion among some British Muslims regarding their personal interpretations of health and disease. A focus on physical health, and attempts at understanding disease states of the heart such as anger, discontentment and caprice in biological terms, or perhaps even more seriously as *normal* human emotions, leaves many in a state of inner turmoil. The 'aches and pains' and 'heartache' so common among Muslims possibly represents an attempt to articulate this turmoil in a form that may be understood by clinicians. Frequent recourse to the diagnostic dumping ground of 'difficult' or 'heart-sink' indicates the miserable failure of many such attempts, exemplifying the difficulty of communicating across and between paradigms. The mass search for 'alternative' or 'complementary' cures suggests that it is not only Muslims that are being left short by biomedicine.[21] By focusing on the external reality, the *corpus*, modern medicine is failing to meet the needs of very many people.

Summary

- An individual's understanding of notions of health and disease arise from a complex interplay between personal experience and cultural factors such as language and religion.
- For communities with a sacred tradition the influence of religious ethic in shaping this outlook is likely to be strong.
- Traditional Islamic teaching considers disease states of two kinds: spiritual and physical. Spiritual ill health is the more serious since the Prophet taught: 'Allah does not look to your bodies nor your forms, but rather He looks to your hearts'.
- Islamic teaching obliges Muslims to seek cures for both spiritual and physical disease. The former are usually sought from those trained in understanding inner realities, i.e. teachers of religion, while the latter are sought from those trained in the physical sciences – many in the Muslim world are trained in both of these disciplines. Cure, however, comes solely from Allah and these individuals and institutions are simply Allah's instruments for effecting cure.
- The Muslim community in Britain is currently in an acculturation phase with respect to its understanding of health and disease.

References and notes

1   Helman CG (1994) *Culture, Health and Illness.* Butterworth-Heinemann, Oxford.
2   Rahman F (1998) *Health and Medicine in the Islamic Tradition.* ABC, Chicago.
3   Lee L (1997) *Breaking Barriers: towards culturally competent general practice.* RCGP, London.
4   Khan MM (1990) *Sahih al-Bukhari.* Dar Al-arabia, Beirut.
5   Ali YA (1938) *The Meaning of the Glorious Quran*, **26**: 87–9 (trans modified). Dar al-Kitab, Cairo.
6   Ali YA (1938) *The Meaning of the Glorious Quran*, **2**: 10 (trans modified). Dar al-Kitab, Cairo.
7   al-Ghazali AH (1923) *Minhaj al-abideen.* Maktaba Isha'at al-Islam, Delhi.
8   ibn Daqiq al-'Eid (1983) *Sharh al-Arabain.* Dar al-Kutub al-'ilmiya, Beirut.
9   Khan MM (1980) *Sahih al-Bukhari*, **vii**: 371–2. Dar al-Arabia, Beirut.
10 Sabiq AS (1989) *Fiqh us-sunnah*, **iv**: 1. ATP, Indianapolis.
11 Porter R (1997) *The Greatest Benefit to Mankind*, p 84. Harper Collins, London.
12 Nasr SH (1997) *The Spiritual Crisis in Modern Man.* ABC, Chicago.
13 Sahih al-Tirmidhi (1996) In: SN Shah (ed) *The Alim for Windows.* ISL Software Corporation.

14   Ali YA (1938) *The Meaning of the Glorious Quran,* **13**: 28 (trans modified). Dar al-Kitab, Cairo.

15   Khan MM (1980) *Sahih al-Bukhari,* **vii**: 395. Dar al-Arabia, Beirut.

16   Johnstone P (1998) *Ibn Qayyim al-Jawziyya Medicine of the Prophet,* p 10. Islamic Texts Society, Cambridge.

17   Al-Halveti TB (1985) *The Most Beautiful Names.* Threshold, Vermont.

18   Rahman F (1989) Islam and health/medicine: a historical perspective. In: LE Sullivan (ed) *Healing and Restoring: health and medicine in the world's religious traditions,* pp 149–72. Macmillan, New York.

19   Surty MI (1996) *Muslims' Contribution to the Development of Hospitals.* Qur'anic Arabic Foundation, Birmingham.

20   Ali YA (1938) *The Meaning of the Glorious Quran,* **5**: 32 (trans modified). Dar al-Kitab, Cairo.

21   Eisenberg DM, Kessler RC, Foster C, Norlock FE, Calkins DR, Delbanco TL (1993) Unconventional medicine in the United States. Prevalence, costs, and patterns of use. *NEJM.* **328**: 246–52.

The Muslim patient

CHAPTER FOUR

The family: predicament and promise

Sangeeta Dhami and Aziz Sheikh

We live in an era in which the nature, function and structure of the family have been thrown into question. Many, for example, would consider an unmarried couple, a single mother and homosexual couples as equally legitimate expressions of the family unit. Islam takes a more conservative stance, arguing that the family is a divinely inspired institution, with marriage at its core. The Muslim encounters with more liberal perspectives on the family have not been without consequence. In the course of this chapter we begin to explore what the family *means* for Muslims living as minority communities in the West. We discuss its strengths, limitations, predicaments and promise. We move on to discuss the subjects of marriage, sex and contraception – issues integral to family life. Our aim is not to be prescriptive, but rather to provide clinicians with key insights needed to allow their Muslim patient's concerns to be adequately *heard*. These concerns, we argue, will often need to be understood in the context of the wider picture, in order to minimise the risk of serious misunderstanding. Case histories are used to illustrate key points.

Family life

One of the most striking features of Muslim society is the importance attached to the family. The family unit is regarded as the cornerstone of a healthy and balanced society.[1] The different plane of emphasis from that found in individual-centred cultures is for many quite remarkable.

Parental rights

On joining the Muslim community, I was quite astonished that so much emphasis was put on my relationship with my parents. Here are a few sayings of Muhammad on this subject to which I was exposed almost immediately:

'May his nose be rubbed in the dust! May his nose be rubbed in the dust!' (An Arabic expression denoting degradation). When the Prophet was asked whom he meant by this, he said 'The one who sees his parents, one or both, during their old age but does not enter Paradise' (by doing good to them).

A man came to Muhammad and asked his permission to go to battle. The Prophet asked him, 'Are your parents alive?' The man replied 'Yes'. The Prophet responded, 'Then strive to serve them'.

Jeffrey Lang[2]

Muslim families – nuclear or extended?

The traditional Muslim family is extended, often spanning three or more generations.[3] An extended structure offers many advantages, including stability, coherence, and physical and psychological support – particularly in times of need.

In Muslim culture, akin to other traditional cultures, respect and esteem increase with age. Elderly parents are respected on account of their life experiences and their hierarchical position within the family unit. It is actually viewed as a gift from Allah if one has the opportunity to attend to the needs of one's parents in their latter years. The extended family serves as a natural vehicle to allow these responsibilities to be discharged. It also provides the opportunity for family values to be transmitted from one generation to the next.

Support networks

A 28-year-old woman consulted with a number of 'aches' and 'pains', suggesting a strong psychological component to her symptoms. Reviewing her notes it transpired that she had had three consecutive stillbirths, the last being only six months previously at 36 weeks gestation. The possibility of the stillbirths contributing to her current condition was raised. This she acknowledged, stating that she had been coping well while in Pakistan, as there she had the support of her extended family. On returning to England, however, she found herself more isolated, and was struggling to cope. The option of counselling was discussed, but was strongly declined. 'What has happened to me is a test from Allah, and something I will come to terms with – counsellors cannot understand this'.

Discharging responsibilities

An elderly Bengali man was recovering in hospital from an episode of pneumonia. He was bed-bound, the result of multiple strokes. On the geriatric team's prompting, the family were approached by social services to discuss a nursing home placement. The family explained that they would prefer to look after him at home. With the support of his GP, and social services, he was able to stay within the family home until his death a few years later.

Challenges to the extended family

In practice, it is usual for the new bride to move into the household of her husband. The change is often considerable and teething problems are common. This transition is all the more difficult where Muslims live as minorities, as in many cases migration patterns have resulted in fragmentation of the extended family structure. Many second-generation Muslim migrants will have grown up in nuclear families, not having first-hand familiarity with the richness and complexity of living within extended family networks. In addition, despite religious teachings encouraging marriage at an early age, there is a secular trend among Muslims to marry late.

Some observers have suggested that increasing age curtails an individual's ability to adapt to change, adaptability being the hallmark of youth. Finally, and perhaps most important of all, Muslim youths in the West are faced with lifestyle choices not available in more traditional cultures. To some, the opportunities with respect to individual freedom offered by a nuclear family structure far outweigh any benefits of living in an extended family.[3]

The challenge of ageing

'Things are not like they used to be. There is an increasing trickle of Muslims entering nursing homes, and I've actually been thinking of opening a home specifically for Muslims'.

Muslim nursing home proprietor

Gender and segregation

Gender issues, and in particular the rights of women in Muslim culture, continue to generate much media attention in the West. Muslim women are often portrayed as inferior beings – desperately in need of liberation from the Muslim patriarchal culture that prevents their progress. Segregation of the sexes, a practice encouraged by Islam, is often seen as proof of the suppression of Muslim women.[4] Although there is certainly much that can be done to improve the position of women in Muslim culture, the stereotype created in the Western media leaves much to be desired. Such misunderstandings are largely due to naïve and simplistic attempts to transpose a Western set of norms and values on to women with a very different history and culture. A detailed critique of the feminist position is beyond the scope of this paper; nonetheless, it is perhaps worth mentioning here that women are considered the equal of men, with the same basic responsibilities under religious law, and importantly, an equal chance of salvation in the hereafter. Islam, however, recognises that males and females are not exactly the same, and on the basis of these biological differences assigns complementary roles to males and females respectively. Those interested in pursuing this subject further are referred to the excellent historical corrective offered by Waddy,[5] and also to Badawi's perceptive reflections on many of the issues with which feminists take particular exception.[6]

Any questions?

At a seminar on trans-cultural medicine, junior doctors were asked if they had any particular questions about Islam. Anonymised responses were encouraged in order to allow the doctors to raise issues of genuine concern without fear of offending the group leader (a Muslim). Two themes dominated: women's rights and fundamentalism.

As already noted, Islam quite clearly demarcates between legitimate and illegitimate human relationships. Societal laws exist to aid the Muslim in abiding by this framework. Segregation exists primarily therefore to minimise the chances of illicit relationships developing. Physical contact between members of the opposite sex is strongly discouraged, though these rules are relaxed somewhat if medical treatment is required.[7] This framework explains why many will prefer to see a same-sex clinician, particularly in consultations necessitating examination of the genitalia. On a very practical note, if recourse to an interpreter is required, the use of same-sex interpreters may offer a considerable advantage. The issue of gender segregation is one that should also be considered when planning health education campaigns, research interviews and other similar ventures.

Barbed wire

Zara, a 27-year-old housewife from Sudan, attended for a follow-up appointment at her local hospital. Her doctor was on leave so she was seen by a locum replacement. On her entering the room, the doctor extended his hand. Zara politely declined, but failed to give her reasons for doing so. The resulting consultation was tense and dysfunctional.

Gender and role demarcation

The male is considered the head of the family – to many a male, however, this is a poisoned chalice, as hand-in-hand with leadership comes responsibility. Economic responsibility for maintaining the family falls squarely on the shoulders of the male, irrespective of whether or not his wife is earning. Unemployment then can greatly affect the integrity of the family, leaving the male in a role limbo. Psychological morbidity in such situations may be high, with ramifications for the family at large.

You earn too much!

Mrs Mu'min attended as an 'extra' towards the end of a busy morning surgery. An accountant, she was the principal breadwinner and brought home a healthy wage. Her husband, a doctor trained in Somalia, was unable to practise his craft, as his qualifications were not recognised in the UK. During the last three years he had been forced into a variety of manual occupations. The reason for her consultation? Confused, distraught and visibly shaken, she explained that her husband was threatening to leave her unless she gave up her job.

Marriage

You are a garment to them, and they are a garment for you.

Qur'an[8]

This short Qur'anic simile succinctly encapsulates the primary aims of marriage – to provide warmth, comfort and protection, and to beautify. Within the Islamic vision children have a right to be conceived and reared in a stable and secure environment; marriage is deemed to provide such an environment. In contrast, celibacy, and sex outside of marriage, are strongly discouraged, as they are considered as behavioural extremes that are not conducive to a wholesome society.[9]

In many senses, marriage is considered the union of two families. The parents, taking into account a range of factors, including religiosity and similar educational, cultural and familial backgrounds, usually *arrange* the marriage. Although the free consent of both the bride and groom are essential prerequisites to a valid union, parental coercion is often strong, placing significant pressures on the young people concerned.

There is some evidence that parents are beginning to better understand the marital concerns of their children. In a national survey in 1975, Anwar found that the overwhelming majority of parents favoured marriage with partners 'from back home'; when the survey was repeated only eight years later there was a fall noted in the proportion of parents supporting this notion. Of particular interest was that in the latter survey a similar proportion of parents and young people were found to be in favour of this custom. The practice of choosing marriage partners from within one's own community, however, continues to be considered important by young and old. In the latter survey, the overwhelming majority of parents, and just fewer than 70% of young Muslims, favoured the principle of endogamy (i.e. marrying somebody from the same tribal group).[3]

Consanguinity

Consanguinity (intermarriage) is particularly common in Muslims of south Asian and Arab origin. Among Pakistani Muslims current estimates are that some 75% of couples are in a consanguineous relationship, and approximately 50% are married to first cousins. This represents an increase from the generation of their parents, of whom only 30% are married to first cousins.[10] Consanguinity confers many advantages, which, at least in part, explain its continued appeal. These include a thorough knowledge of the future marriage partner for one's son or daughter – a particularly important consideration in Muslim minority communities where the usual social networks that facilitate the search for an appropriate partner may be lacking. Because of perceived threats to the extended family, parents often consider a marriage that strengthens existing family ties to be the best guarantee of care in old age. Additionally, the practice allows family wealth to be kept within the extended family.

While there is little doubt that consanguinity results in an increased frequency of familial disorders with an autosomal recessive pattern of inheritance,[11] it is far from easy to assess the relative contribution of consanguinity to the high congenital defect and perinatal mortality rate among Pakistanis. Ahmed passionately argues that the consanguinity-birth outcome hypothesis, that forms the basis of much current health policy promoting cultural change in marriage patterns, is over-simplistic and represents yet another manifestation of ideological imperialism.[12] Usefully, he draws attention to inconsistencies and confusion in the epidemiological evidence linking consanguinity to birth outcome, thus highlighting the difficulties in accurately assessing the relative importance of consanguinity. Other factors of importance in the birth outcome debate that need to be addressed include the high prevalence of deprivation among Muslims, difficulties with access to high-quality genetic and prenatal counselling, and the possible risks associated with culturally insensitive maternity care.[13] Appropriate services specifically tailored to meet the needs of Muslims and other minority groups should be considered an issue deserving priority attention.

Sex and contraception

Sexual norms

Sex in the context of marriage is a legitimate, enjoyable activity – an act of worship that is deserving of Allah's reward. Conversely, sex outside of heterosexual marriage is considered deviant, deserving of punishment in the hereafter.[1] In keeping with orthodox Judeo-Christian teaching, homosexuality is considered sinful – a distinction must be made, however, between a homosexual inclination and the act proper. The former is acceptable, so long as it is not practised.[14]

To argue that sexual promiscuity (defined here as transgression of Sacred Law) does not occur among Muslims, as some would wish to believe, is simply inaccurate. Promiscuity does exist, in all its forms, although in all probability its prevalence is considerably lower than found in some segments of British society.[15] Those who operate outside of this framework will often find themselves ostracised, considered responsible for bringing the family name into disrepute. The prospect of 'coming out' for homosexual Muslims is therefore not a realistic proposition at present.

Despite the very positive outlook towards sex, it is not a subject that is openly discussed. Cultural taboos dictate that sex should remain a very private matter between husband and wife.[9] This explains, at least in part, why Muslims are reluctant to seek help for sexual problems, and the long time lag before presentation to a clinician.

Menstruation

While menstruating, women are exempt from some of the important religious rites, such as the ritual prayer, fasting and *Hajj*. Sexual intercourse is also prohibited at such times. All other forms of physical contact between husband and wife, for example hugging and kissing, are allowed. A period may therefore have a number of social and psychological ramifications. There are also a number of possible implications for clinical care. Women may be reluctant to attend for gynaecological symptoms, cervical smear tests or coil checks, for fear of bleeding following a pelvic examination. Many Muslim women are unaware that traumatic bleeding of this kind is quite distinct from menstrual bleeding and hence the same religious constraints do not apply. Education is needed both within the Muslim community and among professionals so that the significance and implications of genital tract bleeding are better appreciated.

Additional dimensions in the management of genital tract bleeding

A married woman in her late thirties contacted a friend (a female Muslim doctor) to discuss her period problems. She had been bleeding on a fortnightly basis for the previous few months. This was causing havoc with prayer routines, as on each occasion she had stopped praying. She was advised that she should continue praying, as the pattern of bleeding was unlikely to represent menstrual bleeding. It was suggested that she see her GP for further investigation. Thus far she had avoided consultation – contributing to her apprehension were the prospect of not being able to see a female GP, difficulties in articulating the real reason for her attendance and the possibility that an internal examination may exacerbate her bleeding.

Women may consult their GP or family planning clinic in order to postpone their periods at particular times. The most common situation is in the run up to *Hajj*. For those using the combined oral contraceptive pill they can be safely advised to either 'bicycle' or 'tricycle' pill packs. This quite simply involves omitting the seven-day break in between pill packs, thus avoiding the withdrawal bleed that ensues.[16] Alternatively, daily progesterone may be used (e.g. norethisterone), beginning two to three days before the period is due, continuing treatment until such time that bleeding is more convenient.

Female genital tract mutilation

Female genital tract mutilation (FGM) is a practice that is carried out in many regions of the world, including some Muslim countries. FGM is most widespread in parts of Africa, stretching in a band from the Horn through Central Africa and extending to parts of Nigeria.[17] The custom's exact origins are uncertain but it almost certainly predates the arrival of Christianity and Islam to these regions. FGM is currently illegal in many countries, including Britain.[18]

There are basically three types of procedure that are performed, typically around the age of six–seven years. The least invasive of these involves removing only the prepuce of the clitoris. This is the only form that can be accurately termed circumcision. This is also sometimes referred to as the '*Sunnah*' procedure indicating that the Prophet sanctioned this form[19]; Muslims may therefore object to this procedure being categorised as a form of mutilation since the notion that the Prophet in any way condoned acts of barbarism is, for the Muslim, simply nonsensical. Removal of the clitoris or more extensive procedures are, however, not approved of by religious teaching[20]; nonetheless these extreme practices continue in some Muslim regions, largely on account of the strong influences of tribal and regional custom and tradition. The most extreme form (infibulation) involves excising the clitoris, the labia minora and the medial aspect of the labia majora. The sides of the vagina are then sutured leaving a small opening for the passage of urine and menstrual flow.[18] The intermediate form involves removing the clitoris either partially or in total, together with a portion of the labia minora.

The removal of large amounts of genital tissue, as described above, can cause considerable problems, including difficulties with micturition, recurrent urinary tract infection, dyspareunia and dysmenorrhoea. The emotional and psychological ramifications of such a bodily assault are also now being appreciated.

Traditionally, a local midwife will perform a de-infibulation immediately after marriage thus allowing consummation to occur. The recent large-scale migration from Somalia, Sudan, Eritrea and Ethiopia to parts of Europe has highlighted the difficulties and problems involved with caring for infibulated women. Access to de-infibulation is restricted in the UK and women will therefore often become pregnant while infibulated, hindering their care in pregnancy and in labour. Attempts to respond to the challenges posed have been variable,[21] ranging from the *ad hoc* and poorly organised, to those that have developed proactive, structured, high-quality services. One such centre of excellence is at Northwick Park Hospital in Harrow, which has established an African Well Woman Clinic.[22] This centre offers priority de-infibulation either before pregnancy or antenatally. The clinic offers a multi-disciplinary assessment and treatment centre, with access to a translator, a psychologist and a counsellor, all of whom are conversant with the relevant aspects of African and Muslim culture. Mainly female staff are employed – a practice that reflects an appreciation of Muslim sensitivities with regards to inter-gender dealings.

Contraception

Many traditions of the Prophet Muhammad extol the merits of marriage, procreation and fecundity.[23] Muslim opinion with respect to contraception, however, is divided – a minority arguing that it is categorically prohibited, while the majority opinion is that contraception is allowed but discouraged.[24] A small minority, confined largely to academic circles, suggest that effective family planning strategies are essential in order to prevent the global overspill predicted by many in the West.[25] There are wide variations in the prevalence of contraceptive use in Muslim countries, reflecting these divergent views, ranging from under 5% of women of reproductive age (e.g. Mauritania, North Yemen, Somalia and Sudan) to over 50% (e.g. Turkey, Lebanon and Tunisia).[26]

The *British National Survey of Sexual Attitudes and Lifestyle*[27] provides little detailed information regarding patterns of contraceptive use among Muslims and other minority religious groups, categorising respondents as belonging to either one of the principal Christian denominations, a non-Christian faith or no faith. A survey by Gatrad describing patterns of contraceptive use by women from religious minorities in Walsall shows some interesting findings.[28] Categorising women as either Muslim, Sikh, Hindu or European, this survey showed that Muslim women were least likely to report current contraceptive use (Muslim 43% vs Sikh 61% vs Hindu 62% vs European 78%, $p < 0.05$). In a recent survey comparing recorded patterns of contraceptive use between Muslims and non-Muslims, only 21% of Muslims were current users compared with 51% of non-Muslims ($p < 0.001$).[29] Both of these studies suggest that religious ethic has a strong bearing on patterns of contraceptive use among British Muslims. Of interest is that in both studies the intrauterine contraceptive device (IUCD) was shown to be popular among Muslims, following a close second to hormonal methods, despite the increased likelihood of bleeding problems associated with its use. The reasons for the popularity of the IUCD are unclear but may include a number of perceived benefits, such as limited medical contact and the associated decreased chances of needing to consult a male practitioner.

Summary

- The family forms the basic building block of Muslim society. Despite the many pressures this unit faces, the family institution remains strong. The future of the extended family is, however, under considerable threat.
- Female genital mutilation is common among Muslim and non-Muslim women of African origin. Proactive, structured, culturally appropriate care is needed to deal with the complications of infibulation.
- Marriage forms the sole basis for sexual relations and parenthood. The overwhelming majority of British Muslims presently respect this code of conduct. For those who choose to step outside of this framework, support services are scarce and poorly developed.
- Islamic Law generally discourages the use of contraception, extolling the virtues of large families. However, there seems to be a trend towards smaller family size.
- It may be possible to mitigate some social problems such as sexually transmitted infections, cervical cancer and unwanted pregnancies by developing vehicles to strengthen the traditional Muslim family structure.

References and notes

1 Doi AR (1984) *Shar'iah: the Islamic Law*, pp 114–27. Ta Ha, London.
2 Lang J (1995) *Struggling to Surrender*, p 133. Amana, Maryland.
3 Anwar M (1994) *Young Muslims in Britain: attitudes, educational needs, and policy implications*, pp 23–8. Islamic Foundation, Leicester.
4 Goodwin J (1995) *Price of Honour*. Warner, London.
5 Waddy C (1980) *Women in Muslim History*. Longman, London.
6 Badawi JA (1997) *Woman: under the shade of Islam*. El-Falah, Cairo.
7 McDermott MY, Ahsan MM (1993) *The Muslim Guide*, pp 59–63. Islamic Foundation, Leicester.
8 Ali YA (1938) *The Meaning of the Glorious Quran*, **2**: 187 (trans modified). Dar al-Kitab, Cairo.
9 Al-Qaradawi Y (1960) *The Lawful and the Prohibited in Islam*, pp 148–236. ATP, Indianapolis.
10 Darr A, Modell B (1988) The frequency of consanguineous marriage amongst British Pakistanis. *J Med Gen*. **25**: 186–90.
11 Bundey S, Alam S, Kaw S *et al.* (1989) Race, consanguinity and social features in Birmingham babies; a basis for prospective study. *J Epidemiol Commun Hlth*. **44**: 130–5.

12   Ahmad WIU (1994) Reflections on the consanguinity and birth outcome debate. *J Public Hlth Med.* **16**: 423–8.
13   Bowler I (1993) 'They're not the same as us?': midwives' stereotype of south Asian maternity patients. *Social Hlth Illness.* **15**: 157–78.
14   Wayte C (1999) Bible is disapproving of homosexual activity but not homosexual orientation. *BMJ.* **319**: 123.
15   Francome C (1994) *The Great Leap 2: a study of Muslim students.* Middlesex University, London.
16   Guillebaud J (1991) *The Pill,* p 53. OUP, Oxford.
17   Dorkenoo E (1994) *Cutting the Rose,* p viii. Minority Rights Publication, London.
18   Black JD, Debelle GD (1995) Female genital mutilation in Britain. *BMJ.* **310**: 1590–2.
19   Razzaq AB (1998) *Circumcision in Islam,* pp 30–6. Dar Al-Taqwa, London.
20   Keller NHM (1997) *Reliance of the Traveller,* p 59. Amana, Maryland.
21   Oritz ET (1998) Female genital mutilation and public health: lessons from the British experience. *Hlth Care Women Int.* **19**: 119–29.
22   McCaffrey M, Jankowska A, Gordon H (1995) Management of female genital tract mutilation: The Northwick Park Hospital experience. *Br J Obstet Gynaecol.* **102**: 78–90.
23   Hasan S (1998) *Raising Children in Islam,* p 19. Al Quran Society, London.
24   Oberneger CM (1994) Reproductive choices in Islam: gender and state in Iran and Tunisia. *Stud Family Planning.* **25**: 41–51.
25   Rahman F (1998) *Health and Medicine in the Islamic Tradition,* pp 113–18. Kazi, Chicago.
26   Ebrahim AFM (1998) *Abortion, Birth Control and Surrogate Parenting: an Islamic perspective,* pp 27–33. ATP, Indianapolis.
27   Johnson M, Wadsworth J, Wellings K, Field J (1994) *Sexual Attitudes and Lifestyles.* Blackwell Science, Oxford.
28   Gatrad AR (1994) *The Muslim in hospital, school and the community* (PhD thesis). University of Wolverhampton.
29   Sheikh A, Dhami S (1999) *Patterns of Contraceptive Use Amongst Muslims in West London.* UK Federation of Primary Care Research Networks, London.

CHAPTER FIVE

Birth customs: meaning and significance

Abdul Rashid Gatrad and Aziz Sheikh

Over 20 000 Muslim babies are born annually in the UK.[1]
The overwhelming majority of Muslims in Britain, and indeed globally,
will respect the rites of passage recommended by Islamic teaching.
Despite the size of the Muslim community, and the importance attached
to birth customs by British Muslims, few healthcare professionals will
have received any formal training in trans-cultural perspectives and
customs surrounding birth. This chapter intends to begin the process of
bridging this gap with respect to Muslims. The customs are many, and
to the uninitiated may seem unnecessarily rigid and prescriptive – to
those within the tradition they are, however, deeply symbolic, coherent
and complementary. Above all, they serve to remind the new parents
that a fresh chapter is about to unfold in their personal and collective
narratives. To fully appreciate the joy, richness, honour and potential of
parenthood there is a constant need to look beyond the material
dimensions of life.

The rights of the child

O My Lord! Grant unto me from Thee a progeny that is pure:
for thou art He that heareth prayer.

Qur'an[2]

The child's rights over his parents are clearly articulated in Islamic Law. For the most part these are well respected by Muslim parents. These rights begin before conception, stemming back to the all-important choice of marriage partner.

Does a child have rights over his father?

A man once came to Umar (the second Caliph of Islam) complaining of his son's disobedience. Umar called for the boy, and asked him about his father's complaint, and his neglect of his duties towards his father. The boy replied:

'O Caliph! Does a child not have rights over his father?'

'Certainly', replied Umar.

'What are they then?' enquired the boy.

'That he should choose his mother with care, preferring a righteous woman. When Allah blesses him with a child, he should give him a good name and teach him the Qur'an'.

'O Caliph! My father did none of these. My mother was a fire-worshipper. He gave me the name Ju'laan (meaning dung beetle) and did not teach me a single letter of the Qur'an'.

Turning to the father Umar said, 'You have come to me to complain about the disobedience of your son. You have failed in your duty to him before he has failed in his duty to you; you have done wrong to him before he has wronged you'.[3]

Children have the right to be born through a legitimate union, with full knowledge of their parentage. The social experiments currently taking place in some countries facilitating the use of donor sperms and eggs to help barren couples to conceive is, for this and other reasons, categorically prohibited by Islam. The child also has the right to a good name, to be suckled, educated and, above all, to have a loving and caring environment in which he may thrive to fulfil his Allah-given potential.

> **Whither the extended family**
>
> It is a matter of sadness that many children are denied the benefits of not having a grandparent to cherish and dote on them, to take them back on journeys back in time and spin yarns for them. We say again that the trend towards nuclear families is a trend for the impoverishment of children.
>
> AbdulWahid Hamid[4]

Birth customs

The Adhan

It is only proper that the first word that a baby should hear is the name of his creator, Allah. This is to be followed by the Declaration of Faith, *'There is no deity but Allah; Muhammad is the Messenger of Allah'*. Both of these fundamental pronouncements serve as the pivot around which the life of a Muslim rotates, hence their symbolic significance at birth. Both pronouncements are conveniently encapsulated within the call to prayer, or *Adhan*.

The father whispers the *Adhan* into the baby's right ear, serving as a reminder that the father also has a key responsibility in the months and years ahead. Ideally, this should be as soon as possible after birth. The entire ceremony takes only a few minutes, and it is greatly appreciated if parents are allowed the opportunity to perform this rite in privacy.

The *Adhan* ceremony in many ways serves as a metaphor for life itself. Those that have had the opportunity of witnessing a Muslim congregational prayer will be aware that shortly after the *Adhan*, and immediately preceding the prayer, there is a second shorter call to prayer. This second call is the *Iqamah* (Figure 5.1). At the time of birth there is an *Adhan* but no *Iqamah*. For the funeral prayer, however, there is simply the *Iqamah* with no preceding *Adhan*. Our stay on earth is short – the equivalent of the few minutes separating the *Adhan* from the *Iqamah*, so life then should be spent wisely and diligently, and not wasted.

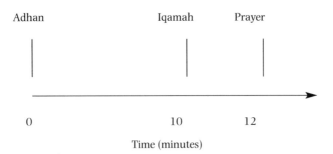

Figure 5.1:   Diagrammatic representation of the relationship between the Adhan, Iqamah and Prayer.

Tahneek

This is a commonly observed practice, which, like many of the others mentioned in this chapter, traces its origins back to the Prophet Muhammad. Soon after birth, and preferably before being fed, a small piece of softened date is gently rubbed into the infant's upper palate. Where dates are not easily available, substitutes such as honey are used. A respected member of the family often performs this, with the hope that some of his positive qualities will be transmitted to the fledgling infant. The practice of only permitting access to partners into the delivery ward has its advantages, but may be seen by some as unduly restrictive, impeding the practice of this custom.

Taweez

The *Taweez* is a piece of black string, with a small pouch containing a prayer, which is tied around the baby's wrist or neck. It is particularly common among Muslims from the Indian subcontinent, with many believing that it protects the baby from ill health. For obvious reasons, it is important that the *Taweez* be handled with respect, and should not be removed or broken except during emergency treatment.

Circumcision

The issue of male circumcision continues to excite a good deal of interest and discussion both within the medical and lay press.[5] Sharply conflicting customs are seen in Western countries, with circumcision being performed on an almost routine basis in the USA,[6] while in

Britain it is a practice viewed by many with suspicion and scorn.[7,8] For Muslims,[9] as for their Jewish brethren,[10] religious law sanctions male circumcision. Female circumcision is discussed in an earlier chapter (Chapter 4). Circumcision is considered particularly important for hygiene purposes, as when the child matures and begins to offer prayers, there is no danger of his clothes becoming soiled from small amounts of urine 'held up' in the foreskin – important because soiled clothes will nullify the prayer. Despite the recent attempts of some Muslim apologists to downplay the importance of circumcision,[11] it seems highly probable that it will continue.

Difficulties involved with obtaining circumcision on the NHS necessitate that it is usually performed in the private sector, at a cost of between £50 and £100. The plastic ring method is most often used, with the procedure performed under a local anaesthetic. Though most practitioners seem to be aware of the need to delay circumcision in jaundiced infants, because of the risk of prolonged bleeding, it is important to remind parents of this. Babies born with hypospadias should also avoid circumcision until a surgical opinion has been sought.[12] Because of the frequency of complications following circumcision by non-professionals, some health authorities have tried to regulate the practice by establishing special clinics for religious circumcision.[13] Others, such as Sandwell Health Authority, have gone one step further, offering free circumcision to males under the age of two years.[14] Such initiatives are very welcome, and deserve to be replicated in other parts of the country.

In the nick of time!

A two-week-old baby was brought into the Accident & Emergency department by his anxious parents, concerned that he was becoming increasingly listless. Further questioning revealed that he had been circumcised some 24 hours earlier. Since then he had been bleeding steadily from his circumcision wound. On examination he was peripherally shutdown, with a haemoglobin count of only 5.5 g/dl.

He was resuscitated, the haemorrhage arrested and an emergency blood transfusion arranged. A private practitioner had performed the circumcision. No follow-up had been arranged, and the parents had been given no advice about possible complications.

There were no NHS facilities for religious circumcision in the area.

Circumcision is usually performed within a few weeks of birth. The Bengali community often delay the circumcision for a few months, preferring the winter period as wound healing is believed to be better. Frequent nappy changes should be advised, together with the liberal use of barrier creams, in order to minimise the risk of ammoniacal dermatitis and the associated risks of meatal stenosis and ulceration while wound healing occurs.[15,16]

Aqiqah

A sheep is offered in sacrifice for every newborn child as a sign of one's gratitude to Allah. This is usually performed on the seventh day and the meat distributed among family members and the poor. Many will arrange for the sacrifice to be performed in their countries of origin, thus allowing the meat to be distributed where there is greater need, while simultaneously enabling disparate family members to partake in the celebrations.

Shaving the hair

A newborn child is innocent, free from the internal failings that grip the majority of humankind – the diseases of avarice, lust, envy and pride, to mention but a few. As a symbolic act, the scalp hairs that grew during intrauterine development are removed, traditionally on the seventh day of life, and the equivalent weight in silver is given in charity. There is another point in time that the Muslim has the opportunity to re-enter this noble state of innocence. The Prophet likened the one that successfully emerges from the standing on the desert plane of Arafat during *Hajj* (Chapter 7), having beseeched Allah's forgiveness for past excesses, as pure, 'like the day his mother gave him birth'. The pilgrim is asked to remove his scalp hair to commemorate this accomplishment.

Muslim names
Choosing a name

As has already been noted, the choice of a good name is one of the basic rights of a child. It is hoped that the name will both inspire self-respect and give the child something to aspire towards in the years that lie ahead. After birth it may be a few days before the child is named, as it is usual to seek the advice, and approval, of members of the extended family. Some examples of common female and male names, together with their meanings, are presented in Tables 5.1 and 5.2.

What's his name?

A young couple were keen to name their first-born Abdul-Khaliq (meaning 'Servant of the Creator'). All family members agreed that the name was pleasant and gave much to aspire towards. There was, however, apprehension that the name would be 'ruined' by those who failed to appreciate its significance, being either mispronounced or shortened to Abdul (meaning 'Servant'). After a few days of trying the name the family's anxieties were confirmed. The name Yusuf (Joseph) was chosen as an alternative – a choice that was met with widespread approval.

Table 5.1:   Examples of common female names and their meanings

Female names	Meaning
Aminah	Trustworthy, faithful
Faridah	Unique
Fatimah	The Prophet's daughter
Nafisa	Precious
Rabiah	Garden
Salma	Peaceful

Table 5.2:   Examples of common male names and their meanings

Male names	Meaning
Abdullah	Servant of Allah
Ahmed	Praiseworthy
Hamza	The Prophet's uncle
Musa	Moses
Sa'eed	Happy
Tahir	Pure

Naming systems

It is in the Gujarati Muslim community, and among Muslims who have their origins in Central Africa and in urban regions of the Indian subcontinent, that the system of naming often follows that found in Britain. Families will use clan or group names as a surname, e.g. Khan or Chaudhry. For many Muslims, however, a more traditional method of naming is used, and it is usually a failure to understand this system that leads to confusion, and occasionally chaos, with GP and hospital records.

Boys may have a personal name, which is either preceded or followed by a religious title, e.g. Muhammad Siddiq, where Muhammad is a religious title and Siddiq the personal name. In the case of his brother, Altaf Hussain, Altaf is the personal name and Hussain (the name of a grandson of the Prophet) the title. For medical records in the UK, the final name is often used as a surname and this would explain why two Muslim brothers might have different surnames! A possible alternative method of recording family names is to use the child's personal name followed by his father's personal name – the latter being used as a surname, e.g. Muhammad Siddiq and Altaf Hussain, the sons of Abdul Rashid, would be recorded as Siddiq Rashid and Altaf Rashid, since Abdul is a title. There are only a handful of titles commonly used in Britain, therefore such a system could be implemented with relatively little training required for record clerks. The potential problems posed by using different names on hospital records and other important documentation, such as passports, driving licences and insurance forms, to mention but a few, would, however, need to be thoroughly explored in advance of any such changes. Anecdotal discussions suggest that there would not be much resistance among the Muslim community to a change of this kind; nonetheless, it is clearly important that the views of a representative group from the Muslim community are adequately sought.

Many Pakistani and Bangladeshi Muslim women will use a personal name, followed by a title, e.g. Razia Bibi or Razia Begum, where Razia is the personal name and Bibi and Begum are titles denoting marital status (Miss or Mrs). A similar practice could be adopted for recording female names, i.e. their personal name followed by their father's or husband's personal name. Razia Begum, the wife of Abdul Rashid, could then be recorded as Razia Rashid (Table 5.3).

Table 5.3: Traditional Muslim naming system and a proposed alternative recording system for use in UK medical records

Family member	Name	Recorded as
Husband	Abdul Rashid Rahman	Rashid Rahman
Wife	Razia Begum	Razia Rashid
Eldest son	Muhammad Siddiq	Siddiq Rashid
Younger son	Altaf Hussain	Altaf Rashid
Daughter	Mariam Bibi	Mariam Rashid

Some help in recognising Muslim names

Muslims are very adept at recognising the names of other Muslims, easily distinguishing them from those of non-Muslims. Usually Arabic in origin – the language of the Qur'an – Muslim names are easily identifiable to the trained eye. For those less familiar with Arabic, title names can be very useful in identifying Muslims. Commonly used titles are Muhammad, Hussain, Abdul, Ali, Ahmad, Bibi, Begum and Khatoon, and therefore any individual with a name incorporating one of these titles can confidently be identified as a Muslim.

Sikhism and Hinduism are the two other major religious groupings found among the peoples of the Indian subcontinent. Both groups often have characteristic names that allow religious affiliation to be easily recognised. Common Sikh names include Kaur, Singh, Gill, Samra, Baines, Uppal, Mann, Khera and names ending in -jit or -jeet. Common Hindu names include Ben, Devi, Kumar, Das, Lal and Patel, although Gujrati Muslims also occasionally use Patel.

Breast-feeding and weaning

Breast-feeding

Breast-feeding is positively encouraged by religious teachings; ideally this should continue for a period of two years.[17] Although Muslim mothers may want to breast-feed, the insufficient privacy offered by some postnatal wards is an important barrier. Muslim etiquette demands that women should not expose certain bodily parts to anyone except their husbands. This includes the breasts, and in order to observe this privacy while in hospital, it is often most convenient to bottle-feed. The trouble with this, however, is that milk production may be adversely affected, particularly in cases where prolonged hospital admission has become necessary. There is a commonly held belief among some sections of the Muslim community that colostrum is either harmful to the baby or that it has poor nutritional value.[18,19] Supplements of honey and water will often be used for the first few days of life.[20] There is no religious basis for this belief. This is an example of a practice that contradicts religious teaching; this dissonance offers a very useful window for the development of educational campaigns directed towards Muslim mothers, with the support of religious leaders and Muslim organisations.

Breast milk from a Muslim mother can be given to another baby but (when older) that baby and his or her mother should be told of this. In religious law, children who receive breast milk from the same person are classed as siblings and therefore, when of age, are prohibited from marrying each other.

Prolonged breast-feeding (greater than six months) is the norm among Bangladeshis.[21] This can lead to iron-deficiency anaemia and rickets if breast-feeding is not supplemented with an appropriately balanced diet. Most Asian families change from an infant formula to 'doorstep' milk at about five to six months.[20] This is contrary to the Department of Health recommendation that states that reconstituted infant formulae should be continued beyond six months in order to prevent deficiencies of iron and vitamins A, C and D.[22]

Weaning

With the exception of Bangladeshis, most Muslim babies in the UK are weaned between the age of three and five months. Proprietary tinned foods are most commonly used, probably more a reflection of the poor socio-economic status of many Muslim households, rather than anything to do with religious teaching.[23] Islamic teaching encourages 'wholesome food'[24] and initiatives could, and perhaps should, be developed, using an appropriate cultural framework to encourage greater use of fresh fruits and vegetables during weaning. This is particularly important in view of the high prevalence of caries, diabetes and ischaemic heart disease among Muslims. Importantly, it is worth remembering that babies are often fed by hand, and children may be positively encouraged to hand-feed. Such a child's spoon-handling skills may be poorly developed – something that needs to be borne in mind if using a spoon is incorporated into developmental assessment tests.

The handicapped child

Many children born with handicaps do not survive in developing countries – thus the care of a handicapped child is a relatively new experience for Muslims in Britain. There is no word in the Urdu language, for example, which adequately explains mental or physical retardation. Parents tend to accept the deformity as an act of Allah, some rationalising it as a 'test from Allah' or as a form of retribution for sins that they may have previously committed. This latter perspective may be seen as a blessing, since it is better to be punished in this world than in the eternal abode of the hereafter. A mother may try to make amends and seek help from a religious leader to effect a cure for the handicap or to prevent recurrences. Unfortunately, charlatans are common and the opportunities for exploitation considerable.

Language problems are a major barrier in the care of handicapped Muslim children because there is a shortage of multi-lingual therapists in areas such as occupational therapy, speech therapy and social work. Parental reluctance to participate in group work/therapy may stem from fear that involvement may publicise the child's handicap within the wider community, adversely affecting the marriage prospects of siblings. Self-help Muslim groups are slowly beginning to emerge, and dialogue between such agencies and professional groups is to be encouraged, so as to allow healthcare professionals the opportunity to hear and understand the concerns of minority populations and fine-tune services appropriately.

Deprivation, consanguinity and the general reluctance of Muslims to abort foetuses with congenital anomalies are key reasons for the high levels of handicap found amongst the Muslim community. Tackling health inequalities remains an important priority for the government, and it is expected that this will in due course bring major health benefits to the deprived. Consanguinity, as discussed in Chapter 4, remains high among certain ethnic groups; for families with a history of congenital anomalies, access to high-quality genetic counselling is essential.[25,26] Where congenital abnormalities are detected during pregnancy, it is important to discuss the possible implications of the findings with the parents (and religious leader if appropriate). This is particularly true for anomalies detected early on in pregnancy, since some jurists hold that termination is acceptable in such circumstances before 'ensoulment' of the foetus occurs – an event that takes place on the 120th day of life. Using religious beliefs and cultural practices in a 'recipe book' manner can sometimes be used as a shield to avoid difficult and painful discussions. The assumption that since Islamic belief discourages abortion, Muslim parents should not be given the choice of abortion is unfair. Rather, this background information should be used as a backdrop against which to explore the wishes of the *individual couple* concerned. Whatever is eventually decided, parents have the right to be supported in their final decision, even if this goes against professional or religious opinion.

Professional imperialism

A recently married genetics student attended the antenatal 'booking-in' clinic in her first pregnancy. A routine dating ultrasound scan was performed which revealed that the foetus had increased nuchal thickness. Suspecting a diagnosis of Down's syndrome her consultant referred her to a tertiary centre for further investigations. Here she was followed up with serial ultrasound scans. It soon emerged that there were a number of congenital malformations, which were considered to be incompatible with life. She was repeatedly advised to have a termination on the basis that it was thought the baby had a less then 1% chance of survival. This she consistently declined, stating that abortion was against her faith. Ultrasound monitoring continued until 34 weeks when she spontaneously went into labour. The baby was stillborn. She was named, buried and is frequently visited by family members.

Adoption and fostering

Adoption involves conferring to the adopted person the status and rights of a natural son or daughter. From the discussion above, natural offspring have rights that predate conception; they also have rights that extend beyond the lifespan of the parents, for example the right to inherit. According to religious teaching, it is not possible for someone to assume parentage on the basis of a simple declaration; adoption then is considered an attempt to deny reality.[27]

In comparison, foster care, being devoid of the legal implications noted above, is strongly encouraged. Fostering is not uncommon, usually between family members, where following an unplanned pregnancy in an already large family, the infant may be offered to a childless couple. Many first-generation Muslims will themselves have first-hand familiarity with being fostered, often with close relatives following the death of parents. If a Muslim child is to be fostered this needs to be with a Muslim family. The Muslim community usually opposes any suggestions of a Muslim child being placed with a non-Muslim family very strongly. We suspect that many other religious groups would on the whole express very similar sentiments.

Summary

- The Muslim child has a number of Allah-given rights; these include the right to be born through a legitimate union, to know fully one's parentage, to be suckled, and to be reared with kindness and respect.
- The traditional Muslim naming system often causes confusion with medical records. This naming system can be adapted to allow family members to be readily identified, though the legal implications and possible logistic problems posed by such a change have not yet been assessed.
- There are a number of birth customs common to Muslims. Most healthcare professionals will have received little training in understanding their meaning or significance. An appreciation of such customs provides a unique insight into the lives of Muslims.
- Male circumcision is an important birth custom. Parents should be advised to delay the procedure in the case of neonatal jaundice and hypospadias. Religious circumcision should be available on the NHS.[28]
- Caring for handicapped children is a relatively new experience for British Muslims. Culturally appropriate support services are poorly developed.

References and notes

1   Pharoah POD, Alberman ED (1990) Annual statistical review. *Arch Dis Child.* **65**: 147–51.

2   Ali YA (1938) *The Meaning of the Glorious Quran,* **3**: 38 (trans modified). Dar al-Kitab, Cairo.

3   Hasan S (1998) *Raising Children in Islam,* pp 23–33. Al Quran Society, London.

4   Hamid AW (1989) *Islam the Natural Way,* p 75. MELS, London.

5   A Medline literature review by the authors retrieved 540 references using the search term 'circumcision' for the period 1990–August 1999.

6   Anon (1999) Circumcision policy statement. American Academy of Paediatrics. Task force on circumcision. *Paediatrics.* **103**: 686–93.

7   Gairdner D (1949) The fate of the foreskin. *BMJ.* **ii**: 1433–7.

8   Black JA, Debelle GD (1996) Female genital mutilation. *BMJ.* **312**: 377–8.

9   Tarazi N (1995) *The Child in Islam,* pp 8–9. ATP, Indiana.

10 Spitzer J (1998) *A Guide to the Orthodox Jewish Way of Life for Healthcare Professionals,* pp 72–3. J Spitzer, London.

11 Siddiqui AR, Dhami S, Ben Hamida F (1999) Complications of circumcision (correspondence). *General Practitioner.* **Nov 13**: 50.

12 Meadow SR, Smithells RW (1991) *Lecture Notes on Paediatrics,* p 194. Blackwell, Oxford.

13 Memon M, Prowse M (1999) Joint working. One for the boys. *Hlth Serv J.* **109**: 26–7.

14 Anon (1997) *The Muslim News,* p 85 www.muslimnews.co.uk/santwell.html

15 Dunn DC, Rawlinson N (1991) *Surgical Diagnosis and Management,* p 448. Blackwell, Oxford.

16 Stenram A, Malmfors G, Okmian L (1986) Circumcision for phymosis: indications and results. *Acta Paediatr Scand.* **75**: 321–3.

17 Ali YA (1938) *The Meaning of the Glorious Quran,* **2**: 233. Dar al-Kitab, Cairo.

18 Lee E (1985) Asian infant feeding. *Nursing Mirror.* **160**: S14–15.

19 Black J (1985) Asian families II – conditions that may be found in children. *BMJ.* **290**: 830-3.

20 Aukett A, Wharton B (1989) Nutrition of Asian children. In: JK Cruickshanks, DG Beevers (eds) *Ethnic Factors in Health and Disease,* pp 241–8. Butterworth-Heinemann, Oxford.

21 Harries RJ, Armstrong D, Ali R, Loynes A (1983) Nutritional survey of Bangladeshi children aged under 5 years in the London Borough of Tower Hamlets. *Arch Dis Child.* **58**: 428–32.

22 Oppe TE, Arneil GC, Davies DP *et al.* (1980) *Present Day Practice in Infant Feeding. Report on health and social subjects,* p 21. HMSO, London.

23 Gatrad AR (1984) *The Muslim in hospital, school and the community* (PhD thesis). University of Wolverhampton.

24 Ali YA (1938) *The Meaning of the Glorious Quran,* **7**: 157 (trans modified). Dar al-Kitab, Cairo.

25 El-Hashemite N (1997) The Islamic view in genetic preventive procedures. *Lancet.* **350**: 223.

26 Salihu HM (1997) Genetic counselling among Muslims: questions remain unanswered. *Lancet.* **350**: 1035.

27 Al-Qaradawi Y (1960) *The Lawful and the Prohibited in Islam,* pp 222–7. ATP, Indianapolis.

28 Bhopal R, Madhok R, Hameed A (1998) Religious circumcision on the NHS: opinions of Pakistani people in Middlesbrough, England. *J Epidemiol Commun Hlth.* **52**: 758–9.

CHAPTER SIX

Managing the fasting patient: sacred ritual, modern challenges

Ahmed Sadiq

The practice of fasting has a long and rich history – it has been used famously to political effect by Mahatma Gandhi, as part of slimming fads, particularly in the West, and also for medicinal reasons such as the pre-operative fast. Above all though, it remains an important religious ritual for many of the major faith groups, notable examples of which include the Yom Kippur fast of Judaism and the Lent fast still observed by some Eastern Christian sects. The Muslim fast of Ramadan, involving over one in six of all humans, is the most widely observed celebration of this most sacred of rituals. With almost 2 million Muslims in the UK, healthcare professionals are likely to come into most intimate contact with fasting when caring for Muslims.[1] After briefly discussing the meaning of the Muslim fast, I consider the rules and regulations governing fasting, using this as a basis to explore the implications of fasting for health and healthcare provision. The chapter concludes with the presentation of four case histories illustrating some of the central issues discussed.

The fast of Ramadan

A blessed month

The month of Ramadan, the ninth of the Islamic calendar, is distinguished above all others because it was during this month, over 14 centuries ago, that the revelation of the Qur'an began. Allah had, in His wisdom and mercy, chosen Muhammad as His final Emissary, responsible for communicating the Divine Word to 'all the Worlds'. Ramadan thus marks the unfolding of a familiar but distinct chapter in religious history; familiar in that the message is a reaffirmation and re-articulation of that delivered by Abraham, Moses, David, John the Baptist and Christ, distinct for this marked Allah's final reminder.

There is an entire literature devoted to the merits of Ramadan, encouraging and exhorting the believers to 'free' themselves from the grip of 'this world'; Muhammad taught that not only are good acts magnified innumerably during the month, but a gate of Paradise is dedicated to the fasting. For the man and the woman in the street then, Ramadan is synonymous with blessing; the flurry of activity through phone lines that follow the sighting of the new moon, carrying the simple but telling message *Mubarak*, 'congratulations' – in that you are fortunate enough to once again partake of its blessings – bears testimony to the importance of Ramadan in the Muslim psyche. The sense of loss that marks the end of the month is real and tangible.

Preparing for Ramadan

You should work only for the hereafter in this noble month, and embark on something worldly only when absolutely necessary. Arrange your life before Ramadan in a manner that will render you free for worship when it arrives. Be intent on devotions and approach Allah more surely, especially during the last ten days.

Abdallah ibn Alawi Al-Hadad[2]

The *meaning* of fasting

Within Muslim ethic fasting is above all a spiritual exercise, serving a range of diverse but complementary functions (Table 6.1). Its central aim is to afford an opportunity to reflect on one's relationships – both with Allah and with one's fellow man. A customary greeting in many parts of the Muslim world, and continued by some British Muslims, is to greet friends and relatives by saying, 'if I have wronged you, please forgive me'.[3] The sense of solidarity engendered by such collective devotion helps to locate the believer temporally and geographically in the fraternity of faith.

Table 6.1: Why Muslims fast

- Teaches the principle of sincerity as a Muslim fasts to please Allah alone
- Cultivates a consciousness of the Divine because a fasting person keeps his fast without any human authority checking his actions
- Develops empathy with the less fortunate through sharing temporarily in their pain and hunger
- Teaches moderation, willpower, self-reassurance, self-control and self-discipline
- Inculcates a spirit of social belonging, unity, brotherhood and equality as it joins together a whole Muslim society in observing the same sacred ritual, in the same manner, at the same time, for the same reasons, throughout the world

The rules of fasting

A fasting Muslim abstains from all food, drink, smoking and intimate relations from dawn to sunset. This is a total and complete abstinence. For those who, through forgetfulness, inadvertently transgress these rules, the fast is not nullified, so long as the act in question is ceased as soon as one realises one's error. There are no restrictions on consuming lawful food and drink between sunset and dawn, but it is considered distasteful to overeat since one of the central aims of fasting is to learn self-control. This self-control needs to extend beyond the material into the realm of social relationships and it is required that the fasting should endeavour to remain unsoiled through avoiding the maladies of lying, backbiting and engaging in frivolous or obscene conversation.[4]

The Islamic calendar is lunar (about nine to ten days shorter than the solar year), therefore, during the course of a lifetime, Ramadan will fall during all four seasons. In Britain, a winter fast lasts on average for ten hours; in contrast, a summer fast may be for almost 19. For those who live in extreme latitudes, where there may be total darkness or total daylight for months continuously, Islamic law is flexible in its application, requiring fasting for the length of time being fasted in a neighbouring region where the normal cycle of day and night is preserved.[5]

Fasting is obligatory on every responsible and healthy Muslim, male and female. Table 6.2 details those exempt from fasting. If a fast is missed intentionally, without valid excuse, then the penalty for each missed day is to fast consecutively for two months or to provide a meal for 60 people.

Table 6.2: Those exempt from fasting

- Children under the age of puberty
- Those with learning difficulties or retardation such that they are unable to comprehend the nature and purpose of the fast
- The old and frail
- The acutely unwell
- Those with chronic illnesses, in whom fasting may be detrimental to health
- Travellers who are journeying greater than approximately 50 miles
- Menstruating, pregnant and nursing women

Fasting and health
Medical exemptions

During sickness, the exemption from fasting may be temporary or permanent. Temporary exemption may be exercised by those patients who have an acute illness where fasting may aggravate their illness and delay recovery, for example those with renal colic whose condition may be aggravated by dehydration, or those requiring antibiotics for an infective episode. Once in good health, the patient should make up for the missed fasts at a later date. A permanent exemption may be applied to the elderly and frail, or those with certain intractable conditions such as systemic cancer, who will therefore not be in a position to make up missed fasts in the future. The chronically ill may substitute their fasting by providing food for the poor.

Islam encourages the maintenance of good health, even at the expense of fasting during Ramadan. In cases where patients are unsure whether it is appropriate to fast due to health considerations, they are encouraged to seek a medical opinion. In cases of uncertainty, a doctor's decision as to whether fasting, or the inability to take medication in the daylight hours, would be deleterious to a patient's health is totally acceptable and should be adhered to (SM Darsh, personal communication, 1995). However, evidence seems to suggest that Muslim patients do not approach their family practitioners in this regard.[1] They may feel that a non-Muslim physician is very likely to prohibit fasting (even when there are no associated health risks) on account of a failure to understand the significance and importance of fasting. In such cases, many choose to adjust their own medication timings to fit in with the times when eating is allowed. A study which looked at the drug regimens of 81 patients during Ramadan found that 46% changed their drug dosage pattern while fasting.[6] This consisted of missing doses, altering the timing of doses, or taking all the day's medications at one time. While in many cases this is perhaps of little consequence, as discussed in the case histories that follow, such practice can at times have serious consequences. Unless taken following medical advice, short-acting agents may lose their effect some time into the fast. In addition, a larger dose taken once daily may have toxic side effects, especially in the elderly. As a rule, it would be far better for patients to discuss medication changes with clinicians in advance of any planned change; this does, however, require clinicians and pharmacists to have an appreciation of Muslim teaching regarding the use of medication while fasting, and also an understanding of the metabolic effects of controlled fasting.

Medication use

Allowing anything to enter through the mouth into the intestine nullifies the fast,[5] therefore any medication that is swallowed will also invalidate the fast. For those who require oral medication, dosage times can usually be easily and safely altered so that tablets are taken before the start and at the end of the fast, or in some cases by switching from short-acting agents to longer-acting ones. Such an approach is particularly convenient for oral treatments for many gastrointestinal, cardiovascular, respiratory, central nervous system, endocrine and rheumatic disorders, as well as for nutritional supplements.

If there is a necessity for the medication during the daytime, for example to preserve life, then the person is considered to be sick and has the dispensation not to fast as discussed previously. For those in whom such a situation arises while fasting, there is no harm whatsoever in abandoning the fast since heroic acts of misplaced piety have nothing to do with the teachings of Islam.

The use of parenteral fluids or nutrition is prohibited while fasting as this involves the use of procedures designed to bypass the alimentary tract, thus having important systemic effects and also being of nutritional value. Agents that primarily have a topical mode of action, such as eye drops, are, however, considered acceptable by the majority of Muslims since jurists have ruled that 'the eye is not one of the apertures leading to the belly'. Although eye drops are not swallowed, small amounts may be absorbed systemically from the conjunctiva and nasal mucosa. Patients who still have reservations, despite adequate explanation, could be encouraged to perform lacrimal punctal occlusion following drop insertion as this will reduce the amount of the fluid entering the nose.

While all agree that the use of oral medications (syrups, tablets, capsules) is prohibited during fasting, the use of other types of medication while fasting is a more contentious area. Most jurists are of the opinion that if a medication is not swallowed but enters into the body or bloodstream, and it is not a source of nutrition, it does not invalidate the fast. This means that while fasting, medication may be taken by all routes except orally. Hence patients are able to take sublingual medication such as nitrates for angina, since these are neither swallowed (but are rapidly absorbed into the bloodstream) nor are they nutritious. This is unlike a substance such as sugar, which even when placed under the tongue, dissolves in saliva and is then swallowed rather than absorbed by the sublingual blood vessels. By analogy, only a minority of jurists allow the use of inhalers for asthma, considering the fast annulled if part of the 'inhaled' medication enters the oesophagus. Skin-patch delivery systems, for example nitrates for angina, can be used while fasting, as again the medication is not swallowed but is rapidly absorbed into the bloodstream. Nevertheless, skin patches delivering nicotine should not be used as the use of nicotine, in whatever form, is not in keeping with the spirit of the fast. Skin creams and other topical medications are also allowed for similar reasons.

Faced with the fasting patient, it is important for professionals to be aware of which treatments the *individual* considers acceptable, and offer treatment accordingly. Though the principles outlined above are shared by all, individual interpretations can and do vary.[7] This should come as no great surprise since many of the treatment modalities discussed had no precedence at the time of the Prophet; in such circumstances Islamic Law requires jurists to consider the issues, using the principles enshrined in the primary sources of law, and arrive at a decision. That jurists may initially come to differing conclusions is expected and indeed welcome – in many cases a consensus opinion evolves with the passage of time.

Implications for health

Most scientific studies investigating the effects of fasting during Ramadan have been performed in Muslim countries. Some of the results may therefore not be directly applicable to Muslims living in temperate Britain, where the risks of dehydration are significantly lower than for those living in the equatorial regions of Asia and the Arabian peninsula, for example. Because of the dearth of local research, extrapolation from available data is made wherever this is considered reasonable. It is also important to be aware that much of Western research on the subject has focused on the ill effects of fasting; in view of the tensions that exist between religion and science in post-Enlightenment Europe this is perhaps not surprising.

Ramadan entails a significant change to the daily routine, with many choosing to spend long periods of the night awake. Modification of the wake/sleep cycle causes an alteration in bodily circadian rhythm for a month; this returns to normal at the end of Ramadan. Meals are taken during the night hours and extra time is spent in prayers and worship, resulting in sleep being delayed and quite considerably shorter than outside Ramadan, especially when the period falls during the longer summer months. Some may catch up with lost sleep during the afternoon or early evening, but this is often not possible for those in full-time employment. This can result in a gradual increase in tiredness and mild sleep deprivation as the month continues. The physical features of fatigue and exhaustion produced by fasting have been shown to objectively reduce cognitive function in some people, as measured by reduced visual flicker fusion.[8] The results of this important study may be extrapolated to other muscular and co-ordination activities of the body which are likely to suffer as Ramadan progresses, especially in the long days of summer when a combination of the higher environmental temperature, sun exposure, dehydration and increased sleep deprivation may all exacerbate fatigue.

In the healthy, normal homeostatic mechanisms ensure that controlled fasting has little effect on body biochemistry. Hypoglycaemia is thus not an issue in non-diabetics for example. In the hot summer days, the prohibition of fluids may lead to mild dehydration, resulting in the common symptoms of dizziness, nausea and headaches, accompanied with a resting tachycardia. The risks of dehydration while fasting may be exaggerated, as shown by a recent study by Abdalla and colleagues investigating the effects of fasting on those who are over one year post-renal transplantation – no impairment in graft function was observed.[9]

There appears to be no significant overall change in body weight during the month.[10] Exceptions may of course occur, and fluid loss may be responsible for any initial weight loss seen in some people,[11] while paradoxically the weight of some people may increase a little during the month. An increased consumption of high-calorific fried foods when opening the fast, common among some, seems the most plausible explanation. Thirst is felt more intensely than hunger, and one tends to feel the cold more, especially when fasting long hours, a consequence of a slowing down of the body's metabolic rate in order to conserve energy stores.[11]

Though changes in serum lipids are variable, there appears to be an overall beneficial effect on serum apolipoprotein metabolism.[12] Changes in meal times also change the normal circadian rhythm for intragastric acidity,[13] resulting in an increase in acid and pepsin secretion,[14] and this appears to be the likely basis for the observed increased risk of peptic ulcer complications during Ramadan.[15] Particular care therefore needs to be taken when advising patients with a history of peptic ulcer disease about the risks associated with fasting.

Although expectant and nursing mothers are exempt from fasting (Table 6.2), many in Britain choose to fast (AR Gatrad, personal communication, 1999). Their reasons are simple, and include a combination of preferring to fast with their families rather than make up the time later when they may be fasting alone and a reverence for the blessings associated with fasting in the holy month. Interestingly, fasting during Ramadan has been shown not to affect the mean birth weight of babies at any stage of pregnancy.[16] Mothers may report that their babies move very little during daylight hours, but this is compensated for by increased activity at night. This is because the diurnal cycle of the foetus changes with that of its mother. Fasting does tend to change the concentrations of lactose, sodium and potassium in breast milk, but the quantity of milk only tends to change during long fasts or fasts in hot countries, due to maternal dehydration.

Although harder to quantify than physical changes, Ramadan appears to have a beneficial effect on psychological well being. Little research in this area exists, but a study of British university students showed that an increased proportion became involved in spiritual and other stress-reducing activities during Ramadan.[17] Another study has found that significantly fewer parasuicides were reported during Ramadan than at other times.[18] Although this particular study was performed in Jordan, it seems reasonable to conclude that one may expect a similar, or an even greater, effect in Britain because of the relatively poor stabilising and protective effect of family cohesiveness in migrant Muslim populations when compared with native Muslim communities. This protective effect of Ramadan may, to the Muslim mind, be explained by the blessings inherent in the month itself, in addition to the more common sociological interpretation of increased family and communal solidarity associated with a common sense of purpose.

Of all research into fasting, that into diabetes is most well developed. Despite the theoretical hazards of fasting in patients with diabetes, in practice few complications occur.[19-21] In fact, fasting may even prove beneficial through weight loss and decreased food intake.[20,21] Table 6.3 summarises current advice for diabetics while fasting.[22]

Table 6.3:   Summary of recommendations for diabetic patients wishing to fast[22]

Diet-controlled

- make the pre-dawn meal the major meal of the day
- space meals equally over the non-fasting period

On sulphonylureas

- if on a single daily dose, take medication with the sunset meal
- for those on more than a once-daily regimen switch the morning dose (plus any midday dose) with that taken at sunset

On insulin

- fasting is not recommended in those prone to keto-acidosis or with wide swings in blood glucose
- if on a single daily dose, change to a twice-daily regimen
- for those on a twice-daily regimen, take half or one-third of the morning insulin dose and take the usual evening dose

Organisational considerations

The epidemiology of fasting

The overwhelming majority of Muslims in Britain choose to fast during Ramadan. Gatrad has shown that over 90% of adult Muslims in Walsall fast, and there is no reason to believe that this figure is any different in other parts of Britain.[23] In view of such high proportions it seems reasonable to assume, when considering organisational issues, that Muslims are fasting. Needless to say, when dealing with individual patients it is far better to ask about individual practices and preferences, where appropriate, rather than assume.

Hospital attendance

Time, considered a sacred commodity in classical Islamic understanding, is of a premium during Ramadan. The poor outpatient attendance by Muslims during the month is thus hardly surprising as non-urgent matters are typically delayed until after Ramadan.[24] In consequence, there may be a small increased demand for acute service provision, reflected in the increased use of accident and emergency departments noted in at least one study.[25] These casualty visits tend to be late at night as patients do not want to receive interventions or treatments that may invalidate their fast.

More interesting, however, is that with appropriate planning and consideration of religious sensitivities it is possible to dramatically improve outpatient attendance rates. Using a complex systemic intervention involving, among other things, the use of multi-cultural calendars by clinic staff,[26] thereby allowing staff to avoid important religious festivals such as Ramadan, Gatrad has shown that it is possible to reduce the proportion of patients failing to attend paediatric outpatient appointments from 50% in 1995 to 12% in 1998.[27]

Primary care

For those working in areas with large Muslim populations, it seems important that general practitioners, nurses and community pharmacists receive some training with respect to managing the fasting patient. As far as I am aware no such provision currently exists. Many Jewish and Hindu patients will also fast at particular times during the year,[1] though the nature of the fast in these traditions is not necessarily identical to the Muslim fast. Such a training programme could also tackle issues and concerns raised by members of these communities. In particular, it would seem prudent to encourage patients to consult their primary care staff well in advance of Ramadan to discuss issues regarding the safety of fasting and any possible medication changes. This may be important for patients who suffer from chronic conditions such as diabetes, asthma, epilepsy, hypertension and psychiatric illnesses. The patient would require review just before Ramadan to ensure good health prior to fasting, and just after Ramadan so that they can either return to their previous regimen or continue with their new regimen if this proved to be preferable or more efficacious. The author knows of one general practice in Nottingham which provides such proactive, structured care.

Case studies

Case 1: epilepsy

A patient was admitted to hospital having had a seizure while driving. Prior to this episode his epilepsy had been well controlled on phenytoin 100 mg three times daily. Observing the fast of Ramadan, which had commenced only three days earlier, he had omitted his morning and afternoon doses, on each of the three days.

Comment
Failing to understand the nature of the Ramadan fast, he was labelled as 'non-compliant', by the hospital staff. Because of the long half-life of phenytoin, he could quite easily have been changed to phenytoin 300 mg taken as a single daily dose. Such a change should ideally have taken place before the start of Ramadan.

Case 2: glaucoma

A middle-aged woman suffering from glaucoma had been prescribed eye drops to be used four times daily at regular intervals. During Ramadan, she wished to fast and so decided to use her eye drops only during the night; in practice this involved instilling the drops only once daily. During the course of the month her glaucoma deteriorated.

Comment
She could easily have continued taking her eye drops during Ramadan as the consensus opinion is that eye drops do not invalidate the fast. Being unaware, without the safety net of proactive, structured care provision, she lost her vision unnecessarily.

Case 3: chronic rheumatoid arthritis

A 54-year-old Asian man with chronic rheumatoid arthritis, well controlled on daily non-steroidal anti-inflammatory medication, consulted his general practitioner to discuss alternative treatment options for the forthcoming Ramadan period. His GP thought it best to switch to suppositories. The patient failed to use the suppositories on the grounds that inserting medication rectally was 'not right', resulting in an increase in pain and stiffness.

Comment
Among many Muslims, as indeed is the case in many other cultures, there is a strong stigma against use of medication per rectum. A more appropriate choice with this patient may have been to switch to a long-acting oral preparation taken once daily with his largest meal. If found to be well controlled at the post-Ramadan review, there would be no harm in continuing with this treatment regimen beyond Ramadan.

Case 4: psychiatry

A woman suffering from depression and other psychiatric problems was prescribed a combination of antidepressants and neuroleptics. During Ramadan she insisted on fasting despite the fact that she had grounds for exemption on medical grounds, and was informed of this by family members. Concerned that a failure to comply with medication might result in deterioration in her mental state, the family took advice from a Muslim scholar who was held in high regard by the patient. The scholar advised the patient that she was permitted to continue her medication while 'fasting'. His advice was heeded.

Comment
This woman was quite rightly advised not to fast as she was exempt due to her psychiatric illness with a very real possibility of her mental state deteriorating if compliance was poor. She insisted on fasting, but was persuaded that taking the medication would not invalidate her fast, which of course it does!

Summary

- While fasting is common to many religious and cultural traditions, healthcare professionals are likely to come into most intimate contact with fasting when caring for Muslim patients. The overwhelming majority of British Muslims observe the fast of Ramadan.
- In the event of a fast posing health risks, Muslims are exempt from fasting. In cases where individuals are unsure of the possible health risks, Islamic law recommends that the advice of a medical practitioner be sought.
- The use of oral medication is prohibited while fasting. However, it is possible, in most cases, to alter preparations and dosage times easily and safely, so that medication need only be taken outside of daylight hours. Medications that are neither swallowed nor of nutritious value do not invalidate the fast.
- Time is considered particularly precious during Ramadan, explaining why a large proportion of Muslims choose not to attend clinic and outpatient appointments during the holy months. Incorporating a multi-cultural calendar into the appointment-booking template should allow important religious festivals to be more easily recognised by clinic staff thereby allowing an alternative appointment to be offered.

Acknowledgements

I wish to thank Dr M Aslam PhD, Head of Clinical Pharmacy, University of Nottingham, for allowing the case studies to be reproduced, and Mr RMC Gregson, Consultant Ophthalmologist, Queen's Medical Centre, Nottingham, for inspiring me to investigate and write on this subject. Table 6.3 is adapted, with permission, from a paper in the *Journal of the Royal Society of Medicine*. Finally, I thank the reviewers and editors for their constructive criticism on earlier drafts of this paper.

References and notes

1 Sadiq SA, Sheikh A (1999) The fasting patient. *Update.* **59**: 639–45.

2 al-Haddad AI (1989) *The Book of Assistance*, p 71. Quilliam Press, London.

3 Waddy C (1976) *The Muslim Mind*, p 9. Longman, London.

4 Abdalati H (1975) *Islam in Focus*, p 210. IPCI, Birmingham.

5 Sabiq AS (1991) *Fiqh us-Sunnah*, vol III, p 166 American Trust Publications, Washington.

6 Aslam M, Healy M (1986) Compliance and drug therapy in fasting Moslem patients. *J Clin Hosp Pharm.* **11**: 321–5.

7 Sheikh A (1998) Medical implications of controlled fasting. *J R Soc Med.* **91**: 453.

8 Ali M, Amir T (1989) Effects of fasting on visual flicker fusion. *Percept Motor Skills.* **69**: 627–31.

9 Abdalla AH, Shaheen FA, Rassoul Z, *et al.* (1998) Effect of Ramadan fasting on Moslem kidney transplant recipients. *Am J Nephrol.* **18**: 101–4.

10 Finch GM, Day JE, Razak, Welch DA, Rogers PJ (1998) Appetite changes under free-living conditions during Ramadan. *Appetite.* **31**: 159–70.

11 Sweileh N, Schnitzler A, Hunter GR, Davis B (1992) Body composition and energy metabolism in resting and exercising Muslims during Ramadan fast. *J Sport Med Physical Fitness.* **32**: 156–63.

12 Adlouni A, Ghalim N, Saile R, Hda N, Parra HJ, Benslimane A (1998) Beneficial effect on serum apo AI, apo B and Lp AI levels of Ramadan fasting. *Clin Chem Acta.* **271**: 179–89.

13 Lanzon-Miller S, Pounder R (1991) The effect of fasting on 24-hour intragastric acidity and plasma gastrin. *Am J Gastro.* **86**: 165–7.

14 Hakkou F, Tazi A, Iraqui L, Celice-Pingaud C, Vatier J (1994) The observance of Ramadan and its repercussion on gastric secretion. *Gastro Clin Biol.* **18**: 190–4.

15 Donderici O, Temizhan A, Kucukbas T, Eskioglu E (1994) Effect of Ramadan on peptic ulcer complications. *Scand J Gastro.* **29**: 603–6.

16 Cross JH, Eminson J, Wharton BA (1990) Ramadan and birth weight at full term in Asian Moslem pregnant women in Birmingham. *Arch Dis Child.* **65**: 1053–6.

17   Afifi ZE (1997) Daily practices, study performance and health during the Ramadan fast. *J R Soc Hlth.* **117**: 231–5.

18   Daradkeh T (1992) Parasuicide during Ramadan in Jordan. *Acta Psych Scand.* **86**: 253–4.

19   Belkhadir J, Ghomari H, Klocker N, Mikou A, Nasciri M, Sabri M (1993) Muslims with non-insulin dependent diabetes fasting during Ramadan: treatment with glibenclamide. *BMJ.* **307**: 292–5.

20   Lajaam M (1990) Ramadan fasting and non-insulin dependent diabetes: effect on metabolic control. *East Afr Med J.* **67**: 732–6.

21   Mafauzy M, Mohammed W, Anum M, Zulkifli A, Ruhani A (1990) A study of the fasting diabetic patients during the month of Ramadan. *Med J Malay.* **45**: 14–17.

22   Fazel M (1998) Medical implications of controlled fasting. *J R Soc Med.* **91**: 260–3.

23   Gatrad AR (1994) *The Muslim in hospital, school and the community* (PhD thesis). University of Wolverhampton.

24   Gatrad AR (1997) Comparison of Asian and English non-attenders at a hospital outpatient department. *Arch Dis Child.* **77**: 423–6.

25   Langford E, Ishaque M, Fothergill J, Touquet R (1994) The effect of Ramadan on accident and emergency attendances. *J R Soc Med.* **87**: 517–18.

26   Gould C, Rose D, Woodward P (eds) (1999) *SHAP Calendar of Religious Festivals.* SHAP Working Party, London.

27   Gatrad AR (2000) A completed audit to reduce hospital outpatient non-attendance rates. *Arch Dis Child.* **82**: 59–61.

CHAPTER SEVEN

Hajj: journey of a lifetime

Aziz Sheikh and Abdul Rashid Gatrad

Ever since childhood, five times a day, many a Muslim will have turned his whole being in prayer towards The Sacred Mosque in Mecca, Saudi Arabia. Journeying to The Sacred Mosque for Hajj (pilgrimage) is therefore no ordinary undertaking. For many, it represents the culmination of years of spiritual preparation and planning. Once completed the pilgrim is given the honorific title *Hajji* (pilgrim). Hajj lasts for five days and as the Islamic calendar is lunar the precise Gregorian calendar dates will vary each year by ten days. Muslims travel to Mecca at other times to perform a lesser pilgrimage called *Umrah*.

Annually, some 2.5 million Muslims perform the Hajj, a figure that continues to increase. Although only incumbent on a Muslim once in a lifetime, many, particularly those residing in the West, will journey far more frequently. In 1999, there were 20 627 Hajj visas issued to Britons, a 27% increase on the 1998 figures.[1] The current figure for Umrah visas stands at almost 29 000. In view of the very large numbers of people, from disparate regions of the earth, and the hostile climate of the Arabian Desert, the chances of disease striking, particularly the elderly and the infirm, are high. In this chapter we explore the significance of the Hajj, describing its rites and practices briefly, before focusing on particular health risks associated with the Hajj, and measures that should be taken to minimise such risks.

The significance of Hajj

The Sacred Mosque (*Ka'bah*)

A curious object, that Ka'bah! There it stands at this hour, in the black cloth-covering the Sultan sends it yearly; 'twenty-seven cubits high'; with circuit, with double circuit of pillars, with festoon-rows of lamps and quaint ornaments: the lamps will be lighted again this night – to glitter again under the stars. An authentic fragment of the oldest Past. It is the *Qiblah* (direction of prayer) of all Muslims: from Delhi all onwards to Morocco, the eyes of innumerable praying men are turned towards it, five times, this day and all days: one of the notablest centres in the Habitation of Men.

Thomas Carlyle[2]

According to Muslim tradition The Sacred Mosque was the first temple erected for the worship of Allah. It stands then as a symbol of monotheism. Many of the rites of the Hajj date back to the Prophet Abraham, one of the outstanding figures in Muslim history. Mecca is also honoured because it is the birthplace of Muhammad, Allah's final Messenger to Man. In common with pilgrimages in other faiths, the Hajj is a deeply spiritual exercise, a journey of heightened self-consciousness and individual self-renewal.

Journeying home

And when, as a pilgrim, he stands before the *Ka'bah* in Mecca (after circling it seven times), the centrality already prefigured by his orientation when he prayed far off is made actual. Clothed only in two pieces of plain, unsewn cloth, he has left behind him the characteristics which identified him in the world, his race, his nationality, his status; he is no longer so-and-so from such-and-such a place, but simply a pilgrim.

Beneath his bare feet, like mother-of-pearl, is the pale marble of this amphitheatre at the centre of the world, and although he is commanded to lower his eyes when praying elsewhere, he is now permitted to raise them and look upon the *Ka'bah*, which is the earthly shadow of the Pole or Pivot around which circle the starry heavens. Although Paradise may still seem far distant, he has already come home.

Gai Eaton[3]

The rites of Hajj

Many prospective pilgrims fail to appreciate that Hajj is physically demanding. It is the most complex of the Islamic rituals and involves, among other things, walking long distances and camping in desert tents, often with only the most basic sanitation.[4] Centrepiece in these activities is when the pilgrim stands on the desert plain of Arafah, from noon until sundown. Here, dressed in the simplest possible garb, standing with people representing a microcosm of our universe, the pilgrim performs a dress rehearsal for the final standing before Allah on Judgement Day.

Because of the sheer volume of human traffic, performing even the simplest rites can take an extraordinary length of time. It is for this reason that there is a religious dispensation for those in poor health[5]; while many make use of this dispensation, some will travel against medical advice – often in the hope of dying in the Holy Land. For British Muslims, however, the situation is more complex; since few health professionals have any awareness of what the Hajj entails, or its associated health risks, doctors typically find it difficult to offer an informed opinion.

Health risks
Problems of sun and heat

Next please!

In the next few days' prostration from (heat) exposure passed at a rapid clip through the hotel. Striking down groups of four or five, it moved from room to room and floor to floor. Soon the hotel began to resemble an infirmary, with dozens of guests in various stages of illness strewn around the lobby every night. Guides were not spared.

Every day the temperature climbed by one or two degrees. At midnight the mercury remained above one hundred Fahrenheit...

Michael Wolfe[6]

Travelling to Mecca in advance of the Hajj is a sensible practice, particularly for those unaccustomed to the oppressive climate of the Arab Desert. It should be remembered, however, that acclimatisation to very high temperatures can take between one and two weeks. There is a gradual increase in sweat production, which facilitates cooling through increased water evaporation.[7]

Sunburn is a significant hazard, particularly for the light-skinned. The recent arrival of large numbers of Muslims from the Balkans, together with the increasing number of indigenous converts to Islam, makes this an increasingly important issue for British Muslims. The use of an appropriate strength sun block is important to minimise the risks of burning, with its associated risk of malignant melanomas. More importantly, it is crucial that sun exposure is kept to a minimum as discussed below.

Heat exhaustion and heat stroke are extremely common, and frequently fatal. The Saudis, in their role as the pilgrims' hosts, do extremely valuable work by distributing leaflets and issuing frequent radio and television warnings of the dangers of sun exposure. The number of people who still succumb to the heat is, however, evidence enough that the message needs to be reiterated at every possible opportunity.[8] Important precautionary measures that may be taken are summarised in Table 7.1.

Table 7.1:   Precautionary measures to minimise the risk of heat exhaustion and
                 heat stroke

- Avoid spending long periods of time in the sun, particularly when it is at its zenith
- Travel by night whenever possible (which may also avoid stampedes)
- Keep heads covered during the day (with an umbrella if necessary)
- Consume large volumes of fluid throughout the day
- Always keep a canister of fluid in your possession
- Increase dietary salt intake or use salt tablets
- Avoid transport in 'open' buses

Heat exhaustion typically occurs in subjects who are not acclimatised and undertake strenuous exercise. Water depletion, or a combination of salt and water depletion, due to excessive sweating is responsible. Water loss can be as much as five litres per day, and up to 20 grammes of salt may be lost. Most cases are relatively mild, with symptoms of weakness, light-headedness and muscle cramps, and will respond to a combination of rest, cooling, fluid and salt replacement. If not adequately treated, however, heat stroke may occur.[7,9]

Heat stroke is a medical emergency (Table 7.2). Skin is hot to the touch and there is a notable absence of sweating. The very young, the elderly and diabetics are most at risk. The extreme rise in body temperature makes prompt and appropriate treatment mandatory. The patient should be moved into the shade, stripped, cooled with a combination of fanning and spraying the body with cold water, and if conscious given fluid replacement, while expert medical attention is urgently sought.

Table 7.2:   Symptoms suggestive of heat exhaustion and heat stroke

• Fatigue, weakness and leg cramps
• Headache, nausea and vomiting
• Giddiness
• Delirium
• Syncope and coma

During the Hajj men are prohibited from directly covering their heads, with a hat or scarf for instance, thereby increasing the risk of direct heat exposure. The usefulness of a quality umbrella, preferably white in colour, so as to reflect the sun away, cannot be overemphasised. Such simple measures may be life-saving if the pilgrim were to lose their bearing in the desert, as is easily and not infrequently done.

Quality footwear is extremely useful, though in our experience, frequently overlooked. During the height of day, the desert sand typically becomes burning hot. Care needs to be taken to avoid walking barefoot because of the serious risks of foot burns. This is particularly important for diabetics with a neuropathy, as very extensive damage may quickly occur, often compounded by the problems of poor wound healing and the increased risks of infection. Those who have not been on Hajj are often unaware of the ease with which footwear can become confused with another pilgrim's and thus inadvertently taken. One may be forced to walk barefoot in an attempt to reclaim one's footwear, with potentially devastating consequences.

Infectious diseases

An outbreak of group A meningococcal meningitis occurred among the British Muslim community following the 1987 Hajj. There were 18 primary cases among pilgrims and 15 subsequent cases among their direct and indirect contacts.[10,11] In their attempt to prevent a further outbreak the Saudi authorities now insist that all pilgrims be vaccinated (Mengivac A+C) before travel. A single dose is required, conferring protection against A and C strains of *Neisseria meningitidis* within five to seven days of injection.[12] Immunity is thought to last for approximately three years. A medical certificate confirming vaccination is required before visas will be issued.

Vaccination against hepatitis A and malaria prophylaxis, together with advice on measures to minimise the risk of exposure, are important. We would also strongly recommend vaccination against hepatitis B (*see below*). In addition to checking tetanus and polio status, typhoid and diphtheria vaccination should also be considered. Many people decide to travel on from the Hajj, particularly to Africa and the Indian subcontinent, and, therefore, as in all travel consultations, taking a full and detailed travel history is important. Pilgrims need to be reminded of the importance of seeking medical attention for any unexpected symptoms, such as fever or diarrhoea, on their return. A persistent cough is also significant because of the reported high incidence of pneumonia (particularly tuberculous) among pilgrims.[13,14]

One of the rights of the Hajj is to have the head shaved, although trimming the hair is also acceptable. Most will choose to have their heads shaved, often in makeshift centres, run by opportunistic barbers. A razor blade is commonly used, and may be used on several scalps before being ultimately discarded. The risks of important blood-borne infections such a HIV and hepatitis B and C are obvious, especially considering that many pilgrims will come from regions of the world where such infections are now endemic. Pilgrims need to be aware of the potential dangers, and need to be educated to insist on the use of a new blade. Physical relationships are prohibited during Hajj, even between husband and wife, and so the risks of acquiring sexually transmitted diseases are minimal.

Menstruation

Menstruation is considered a state of ritual impurity, and hence menstruating women are not permitted to perform the Hajj. This often causes a great deal of concern, an emotion that is perfectly understandable if one remembers the importance of the journey and the time, effort and money that have been invested. Delaying menstrual bleeding, either by using the combined oral contraceptive pill or daily progesterone, is perfectly acceptable, and many women consult their family practitioners or family planning clinics for this reason in the run up to the Hajj season (*see* Chapter 4).

General advice

Contact lenses can be particularly problematic in arid conditions where sand can often be blown into the eyes. Ocular lubricants (e.g. Hypromellose 1% eye drops) should be used liberally to stop the lenses adhering to the cornea. Temporarily resorting to the use of spectacles may be a safer option.

Although there are a number of makeshift dispensaries erected during the Hajj season, these are often difficult to access, largely on account of the human mass. Pilgrims should therefore ensure that they take enough of their regular medication and small supplies of common remedies, such as analgesia, oral rehydration salts and clove oil for dental pain. A simple travel pack comprising adhesive dressings, insect repellent, antiseptic cream and water sterilisation tablets is also useful.

The Hajj travel consultation

Much can be done to minimise the health risks described above, and small-scale attempts have begun in many British cities to provide pragmatic healthcare advice. Increasingly these 'Hajj Preparatory Courses' are advising that pilgrims travel as part of an organised travel group, preferably with access to a dedicated medical practitioner. The Hajj travel consultation (Table 7.3) is now mandatory, since all pilgrims must be protected against meningococcal disease, affording the ideal opportunity to complement and reinforce the key travel messages.

Table 7.3:   Checklist for the Hajj travel consultation

* Fit to perform the Hajj?
* Heat exhaustion and heat stroke
* Foot burns and sunburn
* Infectious diseases
* Menstruation
* General travel advice

Summary

- Hajj, the journey to The Sacred Mosque in Mecca, is a once-in-a-lifetime obligation on all Muslims who are physically and financially able.
- Over 1% of the British Muslim community perform the Hajj each year; this figure is rising rapidly.
- If unprepared, health risks associated with the Hajj are considerable. Most important are the risks of heat exhaustion, heat stroke and infectious diseases.
- All pilgrims must be vaccinated against meningococcal disease. A Hajj travel consultation is thus mandatory, offering the ideal opportunity for health promotional advice.

References and notes

1 Royal Embassy of Saudi Arabia, London. Press Release, 14 April 1999.
2 Carlyle T (1966) *On Heroes, Hero-worship and the Heroic in History*, pp 49–50. University of Nebraska Press, Lincoln.
3 Eaton G (1985) *Islam and the Destiny of Man*, p 242. George Allen and Unwin, London.
4 Sarwar G (1998) *Islam – beliefs and teachings*, pp 78–81. MET, London.
5 Sabiq AS (1992) *Fiqh us-sunnah: Hajj and umrah*, p 5. ATP, Indianapolis.
6 Wolfe M (1994) *The Hadj*, pp 194–5. Seeker & Warburg, London.
7 Clarke CRA, Clark ML (1990) Environmental medicine. In: PJ Kumar, ML Clark (eds) *Clinical Medicine*, pp 756–7. Ballière Tindall, London.
8 Seraj ME (1992) Heat stroke during Hajj (pilgrimage) – an update. *Middle East J Anaesthesiol.* **11**: 407–41.
9 Moxham J, Souhami RL, Walker JM (1990) Physical and environmental causes of disease. In: RL Souhami, J Moxham (eds) *Textbook of Medicine*, pp 77–8. Longman, London.
10 Salisbury D, Begg N (eds) (1996) *Immunisation Against Infectious Diseases*, p 146. The Stationery Office, London.
11 Jones DM, Sutcliffe EM (1990) Group A meningococcal disease in England associated with the Haj. *J Infect.* **21**: 21–5.
12 Salisbury D, Begg N (eds) (1996) *Immunisation Against Infectious Diseases*, pp 147–54. The Stationery Office, London.
13 Alzeer A, Mashlah A, Fakim N *et al.* (1998) Tuberculosis is the commonest cause of pneumonia requiring hospitilization during Hajj. *J Infect.* **36**: 303–6.
14 Yousuf M, Al-Saudi DA, Sheikh RA, Lone MS (1995) Pattern of medical problems among Haj pilgrims admitted King Abdul Aziz Hospital, Madinah Al-Munawarah. *Ann Saudi Med.* **15**: 619–21.

CHAPTER EIGHT

Death and bereavement: an exploration and a meditation

Aziz Sheikh and Abdul Rashid Gatrad

The care of dying patients and their relatives is one of the most difficult aspects of a clinician's job. Enabling an individual to die with dignity can also be deeply rewarding. Providing culturally competent care to the dying requires knowledge and skills – the former in order to minimise the risk of systematic error, the latter in order to apply this information meaningfully to the very *individual* clinical encounter as it unfolds. Islamic Law defines certain expected behaviours at the time of death; our experience, based on witnessing and participating in the deaths of hundreds of our religious affiliates, in many different regions of the world, suggests that these rituals are in the main adhered to by Muslims. Minority Muslim communities, such as those in Britain, face particular problems in observing certain death customs; these will be highlighted together with a discussion of how these difficulties may impinge on the bereavement process that ensues. The highly topical area of organ donation is considered together with an assessment of how Muslim opinion on this subject is likely to evolve in the years ahead.

Death and dying

Every soul shall taste death.

Qur'an[1]

Muslim belief regarding death, suicide and euthanasia

For a Muslim, death marks the transition from one state of existence to the next. Islam teaches that life on earth is an examination – the life to come is the eternal abode where one will reap the fruit of one's endeavours on earth. Death is therefore not to be resisted or fought against, but rather something to be accepted as part of the overall divine plan. Further, death is not a taboo subject in Muslim society and is an area that one is encouraged to reflect on frequently.[2] In counselling Muslims regarding a terminal illness or relatives after bereavement, these points should be borne in mind.

Table 8.1:   The phases of existence

- Life before conception
- The lower world (life on earth)
- The intermediate realm
- Judgement Day
- The Garden and the Fire

Islam views life as sacred and a 'trust' from Allah, thus suicide and deliberate euthanasia are categorically prohibited.[3] Note, however, that undue suffering has no place in Islam and if death is hastened in the process of giving adequate analgesia then this is allowed. What is important is that the primary intent is not to hasten death.

Intent matters

The Prophet (may Allah bless him and grant him peace) said: 'Works are only according to intentions, and a man only receives what he intends'.[4]

The final illness

Considerable distress can be avoided if one is aware of certain death customs that are almost universally practised by Muslims. Ideally, Muslims would wish to die at home.[5] Making death clinical and remote in a hospital setting is not in keeping with Islamic tradition. The dying person will expect to be visited by friends and relatives, who are encouraged to pray for his welfare in the life to come. This is a time when Muslims seek each other's forgiveness for excesses that may have been inadvertently committed. Fifty visitors in the space of a few days would not be exceptional; so strict adherence to the policy of 'two visitors per bed' will cause difficulty for all concerned. Members of the immediate family will often stay by the bedside reciting from the Qur'an, hoping to imbue hope into the heart of a loved one at this most difficult time. Having a copy of the Qur'an on the ward, for those who have not remembered to bring their own, is a kindness. A short passage from the Qur'anic chapter most commonly recited at such times is translated below.

Inspiring hope

The trumpet shall be sounded, when behold! From the sepulchres Man will rush forth to His Lord!

They will say: 'Ah, woe unto us! Who has raised us up from our beds of repose?'

It will be said to them: 'This is what Allah Most Gracious has promised, and true was the word of the apostles!'

It will be no more than a single blast, when lo! They will all be brought before Us! Then, on that Day, not a soul will be wronged in the least, and you shall be repaid for what you used to do.

Verily the companions of the Garden shall that Day have joy in all that they do; they and their spouses will be in groves of cool shade, reclining on thrones of dignity; only delight will there be for them, and theirs shall be all that they could ask for: peace and fulfilment through the word of a Sustainer who dispenses all grace.

Qur'an[6]

The daily prayers play a pivotal role in the day-to-day life of a Muslim, and prayer assumes an even greater role in times of suffering and distress. Family members will encourage the dying to continue with their prayers as long as they are able to do so. Before any prayer, ablution is performed; bed-bound patients will need help in this respect. Muslims pray facing Mecca, which is to the southeast of Britain. Again, for the bed-bound, positioning the bed in the direction of Mecca will simplify matters. Recourse to a compass and prayer timetable would be very useful; a prayer timetable is easily available from most local mosques or perhaps more conveniently now from the World Wide Web (*see* Appendix 1 for details). Many of the visitors and relatives will also need to perform their prayers and it is encouraging to note that hospital prayer facilities are slowly improving,[7] particularly in the major London teaching hospitals (*see* Appendix 1 for on-line information regarding prayer facilities in London hospitals).

Some to Mecca turn to pray

'We asked the family if they wanted their son's bed facing towards Mecca – they were really taken aback, and so appreciative of such a small gesture!'

Intensive care nurse

Death rites

When a Muslim dies the eyes and mouth should be closed and the limbs should be straightened. His body should ideally face in the direction of Mecca. It is a religious requirement that the dead be buried as soon as possible and considerable family distress can be avoided by speedy production of the death certificate. The body will be washed and shrouded in simple, unsewn pieces of white cloth – a familiar garb – this having previously been worn as a pilgrim during Hajj while standing on the desert plane of Arafat (*see* Chapter 7). A funeral prayer is held in the local mosque and family and community members follow the funeral procession to the graveyard, where a final prayer is said as the deceased is finally laid to rest, facing towards Mecca. Events occur in rapid succession and in many cases the dead will be buried, particularly in the Muslim countries, within hours of death.

Accommodating diversity: the British experience

Two practical questions have arisen for local authorities out of these requirements, namely availability of space in cemeteries allowing the required alignment, and availability of graves at short notice. The solution adopted in most instances has been the allocation of special areas within cemeteries for Muslim burial, a practice which also meets with the community's understandable wish to have Muslims buried in close proximity to each other.

Jorgen Nielsen[8]

A framework for understanding Muslim bereavement

The subject of Muslim bereavement has received little attention in the biomedical literature. Important questions thus remain with regard to bereavement service provision, particularly since in some quarters it is now argued that primary care staff should provide routine, protocol-driven, bereavement care.[9] It is not clear to what degree the various bereavement models currently in vogue are applicable to Muslims, for example, or whether data from cohort studies showing the often-striking association between recent bereavement and subsequent psychological and physical morbidity are applicable to Muslims.[10,11] Our experience suggests that both the above observations appear to have limited face validity with respect to Muslims. Notwithstanding the need for further research, described below is a framework allowing loss and bereavement to be understood from *within* the Muslim tradition. This, we feel, more accurately allows an appreciation of Muslim experiences of bereavement.

Homeward bound

It has already been noted that life has many phases, the hereafter being a palpable reality within the Islamic vision. Within such a framework, the inevitable sense of loss that occurs at the time of death is tempered by the belief that any separation is temporary. Furthermore, there is solace in the knowledge that traversing the bridge of death enables the deceased to re-enter his ancestral home, returning to the Highest Company.

A traveller's prayer

O Allah, make the end of my life the best of my life, and the best of my deeds, their conclusion, and the best of my days, the day on which I shall meet Thee.

O Allah, make death the best of the things we chose not, but which we await; and the grave the best dwelling in which we shall dwell – and, then death, make best that which follows death.

Ahmad Kamal[12]

The difficult test

Of a surety we will test you with something of fear and hunger, loss of life, or the fruits of your toil. But give glad tidings to those who patiently persevere.

Qur'an[13]

The Qur'an repeatedly asserts that life is a test. It makes no pretence that the trials and tribulations that life has to offer are significant and, at times, difficult to bear; we are also reminded that in all cases these are surmountable. Undoubtedly one of the most distressing experiences for any individual is the loss of a loved one. However, loss need not be a completely negative experience as it represents an occasion to reflect on social and spiritual relationships, and indeed on the purpose and meaning of life itself. A Sufi master will speak of bereavement as offering the opportunity to reach the station of *Sabr* – an Arabic term that denotes the state of constant and unconditional contentment with the Divine decree. *Sabr* represents one of the greatest heights of spiritual development that a Muslim can attain. It is this quality that the bereaved family will be encouraged to practise and develop by fellow community members. Perhaps unsurprisingly, not all practices conform to religious dictates; for example, Islam strongly prohibits wailing following death, yet the practice continues in many quarters. This pre-Islamic custom that originally existed to express the sense of loss felt perhaps continues as a vehicle to inform fellow community members that their support will be needed in the weeks and months ahead.

Loss of offspring, irrespective of their stage of development, is a most trying experience. Here, in addition to encouraging *Sabr*, community members will attempt to comfort the bereaved by reminding them that children are pure and innocent and therefore are assured of paradise.

Radio ga ga

Caller: 'What about a woman who has a miscarriage? Some people say that – well, you shouldn't get too upset, because the loss isn't real – it's not like the death of a child'.

Panellist: 'The pain and loss can be very real, as couples see their hopes fade away. We should be sensitive, recognising the difficulty of the situation. For those who remain resolute, thinking good of Allah, there is the deeply comforting tradition of the Prophet (may Allah bless him and grant him peace):

By Him in whose hand is my soul, the miscarried foetus draws its mother into Paradise by its umbilical cord, when she seeks her reward (for the loss) from Allah.'

Radio Ramadan

Dear Uncle

We here, so many miles away, are with you, in this difficult hour. You *must* remember, my dearest uncle, that what has happened is by Allah's decree – a plan that we cannot always understand. As for Sami, he is now free, having escaped the difficulties of this world; it is as if we can see him – laughing, playing, with that cheeky grin – rejoicing in his new home, his *real* home. We must wait patiently for the time when we too will finally join him – that final union. Your pain, our pain, Allah knows is real – but, dear uncle, take solace in the words of our Prophet (may Allah bless him and grant him peace):

When a child of a servant of Allah passes away, Allah says to the angels: 'Did you take away the apple of My servant's eye?' They reply: 'Yes.' He, the Almighty then asks: 'What did My servant say?' They say: 'He praised you and said: "Unto Allah we belong and unto Allah will we return". At this Allah says: 'Build for My servant a mansion in Paradise – and call it the House of Praise'.

Sami died suddenly and unexpectedly, aged six

An activist model

The immediate pre- and post-death rituals encourage a 'hands-on' approach to dying and death. Close relatives and friends will typically participate in the physical and spiritual care of the dying, and take a lead role in organising and performing the post-death rites of washing, shrouding and burying the deceased. Ensuring that these rights are performed in a quick, efficient and dignified manner is an important consideration for the family and will occupy much of the initial post-death period. The prescribed rituals during this period provide great stability at a time that has the potential to cause much disorientation; the active involvement in the care of the deceased ensures that the feelings of numbness and denial described by Bowlby in his phase model of bereavement are unusual among Muslims.[14]

Comforting thoughts

'Whenever I stopped reciting (from the Qur'an), she would rouse somewhat, as if to say "Carry on! Don't stop!" She died peacefully – whilst I recited'.

Schoolteacher, reflecting on the death of his mother

Mourning is usually for three days during which community members will visit the household of the deceased. Two or three hundred visitors during this time is not unusual. The mood is serious and reflective, yet one in which positive aspects of the deceased's personal narrative are freely and frequently expounded. Formal and informal prayers for the individual's welfare in the life to come are a central theme; visitors will also pray that immediate family members be blessed with achieving the station of *Sabr*. The community support available means that recourse to medical services is infrequently needed. The traditional supportive role of medical staff in such situations may thus be inadvertently challenged, resulting in feelings of unease and alienation on the part of the doctor (B Hurwitz, personal communication, 1998). Understanding of Muslim death customs should prevent such a response occurring.

In the case of widows, the mourning period is approximately 19 weeks, by which time it should be apparent if the widow is carrying her husband's offspring. The period of mourning for a pregnant woman terminates on delivery, irrespective of the time duration since her husband's death. In our experience, this requirement is usually respected, with women remaining primarily within the marital home. Many, however, are unaware of the religious dispensation allowing travel for seeking medical care, resulting in poor attendance for clinic appointments. A proactive, yet flexible, approach to dealing with this issue is to be encouraged. In most cases, it should be possible to offer a more convenient appointment. Where delay is detrimental, education regarding the religious obligation to seek medical attention (perhaps using leaflets written in conjunction with local religious leaders) and greater use of domiciliary services are the key.

Enduring relationships

Within some philosophies, death marks the end. For the adherents of such a philosophy, death will also mark the end of relationships that were once enjoyed. Islam takes a radically different view, for not only do relationships continue, it is considered possible to assist the deceased in their further journeying. This honouring of the deceased is a value that many Muslims nurture from early childhood, such as regularly visiting graveyards where loved ones have been laid to rest. The greeting used on entering the graveyard, *Assalamu-Alaikum* meaning 'peace be with you', is the same as that used to greet the living. The prayer that follows emphasises the fact that reunion will take place.

Waiting patiently

On entering a graveyard the Prophet (may Allah bless him and grant him peace) recommended the following words:

'Peace be with you, O you dwellers of these abodes – believers and Muslims. May Allah have mercy on those of you who were first to die and those who were last. We will, whenever Allah wills, join you. I beseech Allah for salvation for you and us'.[15]

If the deceased had any outstanding religious obligations, such as the pilgrimage to Mecca (Hajj) family members will try to fulfil these requirements on their behalf. Also considered important is the need to maintain relationships and friendships that the individual enjoyed when alive. Perpetuating social networks of this kind has also been shown to be important to primary care medical staff. Finally, it is important to be aware that the deceased can be credited with good after leaving this world.

Family and friends, by contributing to such metaphysical memorial funds, have the opportunity to make an enduring legacy to a loved one, wherever and whenever they feel the need.

Recurrent Hajj syndrome

Nazir, a middle-aged accountant, made preparations for his fourth Hajj (pilgrimage to Mecca) in as many years. Having completed his own, he had performed the sacred rite on behalf of his late parents, they themselves not having had the means to make the journey during their lifetime. One debt now remained – Hajj on behalf of his grandfather.

Post-mortems and organ transplants

For novel matters that are not explicitly dealt with in Islamic Law, Muslim jurists are required to study the issue in question and using the principles enshrined within the Qur'an and *Hadith* arrive at a legal opinion, known as a *Fatwa*. It is important to appreciate that a *Fatwa* is an opinion and therefore not binding; thus one can expect a broad range of views on a given question. This is the case with post-mortem examinations and organ transplantation.

The majority opinion is that post-mortem examinations are not allowed. The reasons for this include the fact that the post-mortem will inevitably delay the burial. Second, Islamic belief holds that it may be possible for the deceased to still perceive pain. This is based on the statement of the Prophet Muhammad that 'to break the bone of a dead person is like breaking the bone of a living person'.[16]

Where the law of the land demands post-mortem examinations, i.e. at the coroner's request, Muslims have no choice but to comply. In this case, informing the coroner's officer that the deceased is a Muslim may speed up the process, as many coroners are now aware of Muslim sensitivities. There is, however, the wider issue of whether the coroner's service is in need of reform so that it more accurately reflects the diversity of opinion on post-mortem examinations found in modern-day pluralist Britain.[17] Having first-hand experience of the intense pain and suffering that such state intrusions may cause, we would very strongly urge that the criteria for compulsory post-mortem for Muslims, and perhaps also the Orthodox Jewish community, be restricted to those cases in which there is a genuine medico-legal need.[18] For post-mortem examinations that clinicians consider desirable for educational or other purposes, it is important that it is made explicit that family members have a free choice in the matter, and that their views will be respected.

With respect to organ transplants opinion is more divided. For the reasons cited above, many oppose the donating of organs. Further it is argued that since life is a 'trust', one has no right to 'donate' any part of one's body to someone else. This view is particularly common among Muslims of Asian origin. An increasing number of Muslims, however, are of the view that in cases where organ donation may save life then it is allowed, even desirable, on the basis of the Islamic doctrine that 'necessity allows the prohibited'. An important *Fatwa* from the UK-based Muslim Law (*Shariah*) Council in 1995 was strongly supportive of Muslims donating organs, and deserves wider circulation and debate.[19] It is our opinion that this ruling will have widespread appeal, particularly among second- and third-generation British Muslims, and will in time lead to a greater willingness to organ donate.

At a practical level we suggest that discussions concerning organ transplantation are initiated by the transplant team, included in which should be personnel familiar with Muslim anxieties, allowing these concerns to be addressed accurately and sensitively. Such liaison workers may also have a key role to play in the aftermath of organ donation or transplant, exploring and allaying any feelings of guilt that may ensue.

Summary

- Muslim death and bereavement customs are strongly shaped by religious teachings; an understanding of this narrative is important to allow care to be appropriately delivered.
- Family members are strongly encouraged to participate in the care of the dying; where possible Muslims should be allowed and encouraged to take a 'hands-on' approach to the care of dying friends and relatives. Relaxation of hospital visiting regulations would facilitate this.
- A quick burial is encouraged. Barriers to this include delay in having death certificates issued and registering the death, the need for post-mortem examinations, and difficulties in burying the deceased at weekends and on public holidays.
- Difficulties in observing death rites are likely to have detrimental effects on the bereavement process that ensues; Muslim bereavement remains an under-researched area.
- On organ transplantation, the Muslim community in Britain expresses mixed views. Any campaign aimed at encouraging organ donation by Muslims should reflect an appreciation of Islamic teaching on the subject.

Acknowledgements

Some of the material in this chapter has been reproduced, with permission, from a paper published in the *Journal of the Royal Society of Medicine* [Sheikh A (1998) Death and dying – a Muslim perspective. *J R Soc Med.* **91**: 138–40].

References and notes

1   Ali YA (1938) *The Meaning of the Glorious Quran*, **2**: 185 (trans modified). Dar al-Kitab, Cairo.
2   al-Ghazali AH (1995) *The Remembrance of Death and the Afterlife*. Islamic Texts Society, Cambridge.
3   Sheikh A (1998) Death and dying – a Muslim perspective. *J R Soc Med.* **91**: 138–40.
4   an-Nawawi (1976) *Forty Hadith*, p 26. The Holy Koran Publishing House, Damascus.
5   Gatrad AR (1994) Muslim customs surrounding death, bereavement, postmortem examinations, and organ transplants. *BMJ.* **309**: 521–3.

6   Ali YA (1938) *The Meaning of the Glorious Quran*, **36**: 51–8 (trans modified). Dar al-Kitab, Cairo.
7   Sheikh A (1997) Quiet room is needed in hospitals for prayer and reflection. *BMJ.* **315**: 1625.
8   Nielsen JS (1988) Muslims in Britain and local authority responses. In: T Gerholm, YG Lithman (eds) *The New Islamic Presence in Western Europe*. Mansell, London.
9   Charlton R, Dolman E (1995) Bereavement: a protocol for primary care. *Br J Gen Pract.* **45**: 427–30.
10   Woof WR, Carter YH (1997) The grieving adult and the general practitioner: a literature review in two parts (part 1). *Br J Gen Pract.* **47**: 443–8.
11   Woof WR, Carter YH (1997) The grieving adult and the general practitioner: a literature review in two parts (part 2). *Br J Gen Pract.* **47**: 509–14.
12   Kamal A (1964) *The Sacred Journey*, p 32. Allen and Unwin, London.
13   Ali YA (1938) *The Meaning of the Glorious Quran*, **2**: 155–7 (trans modified). Dar al-Kitab, Cairo.
14   Bowlby J (1983) *Loss: sadness and depression. Attachment and loss*, vol 3. Basic Books, New York.
15   Cited in: Badawi J (1993) *Selected Prayers*, pp 60–1. Ta Ha, London.
16   al-Asqalani AIH (1996) *Bulugh al-Maram*, pp 199–200. Dar-us-Salam Publications, Riyadh.
17   Sheikh A, Gatrad AR, Dhami S (1999) Culturally sensitive care for the dying is a basic human right. *BMJ.* **319**: 1073.
18   Pounder D (1999) The coroner service. *BMJ.* **318**: 1502–3.
19   Anon (1996) The Muslim Law (Shariah) Council and organ transplants. *Accid Emerg Nurs.* **4**: 73–5.

CHAPTER NINE

Conclusions: breaking barriers, building bridges

Aziz Sheikh and Abdul Rashid Gatrad

Religion and health share a rich and intricate past; their present inter-relationship is arguably all the more intriguing. For not only do they meet at the great turning points of life, the junctures of birth and death, but religion continues to profoundly influence and shape notions of health and disease for very many people. '*Omnis natura Deo loquitur*' (the whole of nature speaks of God)[1] is the framework within which the man of faith sees the universe around him; matters to do with health must of necessity then fall within the scope of this world-view. In this work we have sought to build on the growing corpus of academic and lay writing on the interface between faith and health by focusing attention on the traditions, experiences, hopes and concerns of Muslims – Britain's and Western Europe's largest religious minority. An appreciation of Islam, and its central narrative, then is vital to understanding these peoples and the ways in which they experience and comprehend this sacred interface.

But understanding Islam, for the Western educated health professional at least, is difficult. When seeking to relate to his Muslim patient important barriers stand in his way. First, there is the problem of institutional racism embedded firmly within British culture.[2] The British Home Secretary, The Right Honourable Jack Straw MP, recently acknowledged that the National Health Service is 'a long-established, white-dominated organisation (which) is liable to have procedures, practices and a culture that tend to exclude or to disadvantage non-white people'.[3] The net effect is that healthcare professionals will typically have ingrained within them, often subconsciously, the belief that the lifestyles and mannerisms of coloured peoples are inferior to those of the white majority.[4]

There is in addition the difficulty of how, and to what degree, those educated in a secular biomedical model of healthcare, which takes as its starting point Parkin's 'spiritless cadaver',[5] can relate to and understand those who bring with them very different notions of existence. As post-Renaissance man lost his integrated vision of existence, he chose to concentrate his energies and enquiries on the physical and material. Reduced to an accident of history, he turned outwards in search of fulfilment. Natural then that science, now synonymous with domination, mastery and exploitation of the earth and her resources, should rise to a position of supreme importance.[6–8] Medicine retained an important position within the mechanistic universe rapidly being constructed,[9,10] its role now though very different, for no longer was it engaged in delivering the 'holism' of the Semitic faiths or the 'balance' of the Taoist. Rather, it had now become pitted in battle – the battle for survival.[11] Any remnants of belief about matters transcendent became, and remain, coloured with the immutable dichotomy of 'sacred' and 'mundane'.

Being faced with Muslims who have never recognised such divisions is therefore challenging and complex. For theirs is a vision that acknowledges the tri-partite nature of man, comprising *spiritus*, *anima* and *corpus*, and one in which unity reigns supreme. This unity they see extending beyond their immediacy, finding resonance in the world around them. Charged with fulfilling the time-honoured role of trustee and custodian, all is, and must be, 'sacred'.

And then there is the widespread and pernicious problem of Islamophobia.[12] A millennium of hostilities directed against Muslims and their religion has not been without consequence.[13,14] Dismissed initially as a 'heretical faith', the Western powers maintained that Muhammad was 'cruel and crafty, lustful and ignorant', motivating his followers through the 'crude outpourings of the Koran'. The Oriental attack took on a more subtle tone during the imperialist era arguing that although Muhammad was 'undoubtedly sincere' it must nonetheless be concluded that it was his religion that was responsible for the 'backwardness' of Muslims *vis-à-vis* their colonial rulers.[15] The attacks continue almost unabated, the tried and trusted headline of an

'Islamic bomb', or yet another 'Muslim fundamentalist on the killing rampage', enticement enough it seems for those obsessed with feeding past prejudices. Little wonder then that almost endemic within British society are the beliefs that Islam denigrates women, is anti-progressive, and a religion of terror and extremism. The global 'threat from Islam' is thus to many a Western mind both real and imminent.[16]

The all-too-familiar stories of misunderstanding, prejudice and discrimination that we have heard testify to the difficulties that lie in the path of those wishing to deliver culturally competent and sensitive care. Take for example the Turkish bookseller who, after his wife had been delivered of their third and 'final' child by caesarean section, asked if Islam was really so despised by 'the West' that the surgeon's knife had too been recruited in the battle to curb Muslim numbers. Or the elderly Afghani, on being made aware of the animal gelatine component of the antibiotic capsules he had been prescribed, asked how his general practitioner could have made such an important mistake. Or the middle-aged Kenyan car mechanic who, wiping a tear from his eye, inquired why the medical profession had subjected his elderly mother to the pains of a post-mortem – was the caring profession really so insensitive?

But despite the sorry picture painted, and the barriers identified, our prognosis is not necessarily bleak. For those who see a need to bridge gulfs there must always exist certain rays of hope. Take for example, the burgeoning medical interest in issues to do with race, ethnicity and culture that have led to the development of a range of new and exciting disciplines – transcultural medicine[17–19] and medical anthropology[20] for example – dedicated to investigating the impact of such factors on issues to do with health. It must, however, be admitted that these subjects are as yet in their infancy, and their role in shaping medical education, research, clinical care and health policy remains marginal.

There is too a growing belief that despite all its breathtaking successes the reductionism that characterises biomedicine impoverishes our conception of human beings. Through focusing on only the temporal side of man, and in seeking to conquer rather than concur with nature, it is suggested that modern medicine has severed its links with the health beliefs of a diverse array of cultures and almost all health belief models constructed hitherto.[21] For whether we choose to study Indian Vedic medicine,[22] ancient Chinese medicine,[23,24] or indeed the medicine of Antiquity,[25] from which biomedicine claims its origins, notions of spirituality and the metaphysical dimension of existence have figured strongly. The once lone voice of Nasr,[26,27] the brilliant exponent of traditionalism, asserting that medicine needs to 'rediscover the anatomy of being', is it seems gaining momentum and wider acceptance.

In the United States in particular, it now appears that a *vox populi* has begun to make itself heard arguing for more explicit connections between religion and health to be re-established.[28,29] Research suggests that public belief in the benefits to health of religious faith and practices are high. Also noteworthy is that there is some evidence to suggest that a smaller, though significant, proportion of the medical community may also subscribe to this view. For example, of 296 physicians surveyed during the 1996 American Academy of Family Physicians meeting, 99% were of the opinion that religious beliefs can have healing effects, and over 70% were of the opinion that the prayers of others could help a patient's recovery.[28] The subsequent religion–health outcome debate that is currently afoot in America sends ripples of uncertainties through those who had, so they thought, buried religion once and for all.

Outcome measures considered have thus included indices of psychological well being, where much of the work to date has been concentrated,[30] and lifestyle factors important to health such as cigarette consumption,[31] alcohol consumption[32] and marital status.[33] Not surprisingly perhaps, religious involvement has been shown to have a health protective role, being associated with a lower risk of mental health problems and a lifestyle favourable to promoting health. More recently, interest has begun to focus on the effects of religious practice on physical health. Here, once again, evidence points in favour of religious practice being associated with a diverse array of health benefits, such as better obstetric outcome,[34] lower blood pressure,[35] reduced risk of cancer[36] and increased overall life expectancy.[33,37–40]

Some of these health benefits may in part be explained by factors such as differing demographics, health habits and social support among the religiously active. Nonetheless, the benefits to health are shown on balance to persist in studies that have attempted to control for such potential confounding factors. Further, early work exploring the impact of religion on health service utilisation also seems to suggest a close relationship between the two, with lower consulting rates, lower hospital admission rates and decreased length of hospital stay among those who express a religious commitment.[41,42]

We also take comfort from recent positive soundings from the Council of Europe, re-emphasising that patients have a right to have their religious beliefs respected. Such positive sentiments are also central to

The Patient's Charter,[43] finding echoes in the principles embedded within the General Medical Council guidelines *Duties of a Doctor*[44] and in the writings of Hancock,[45] General Secretary of the Royal College of Nursing. The government's commitment that the next decennial census will for the first time ask about religious affiliation, the greater willingness of research charities and biomedical journals to fund and report research to do with matters religious, and the willingness from the Department of Health to support and work with faith groups,[46] suggest to us that religion is set to assume a more culturally civic position among the medical profession. While the proposition that the 'wall of separation' between religion and medicine may soon be demolished seems somewhat premature,[47] it is clear that the long-standing dialogue between religion and health still has much to offer.

As Europe come to terms with its past, there is a greater willingness from the British establishment to promote dialogue and discussion with Muslims about relationships between Muslims and the West. Fundamental differences in outlook may of course exist, but this should not prevent either community from recognising the very many points of similarities – the common Judeo-Christian origin of our societies, our respect for learning and the institutions of the family to mention but a few examples. The positive calls for dialogue from the likes of HRH The Prince of Wales,[48] the British Prime Minister[49] and members of his cabinet[50,51] have also provided cause for optimism.

Most reassuring of all, however, are those small gestures – the kind midwife who after delivering the young Indian accountant of her first-born asks 'Can I cover you?', the offer of NHS circumcision displayed on the paediatric ward notice board, the water jug in the surgery lavatory, those touching electronic *Eid* cards from colleagues and a Secretary of State for Health greeting his Muslim audience with '*Assalamu-Alaikum*'.[52] Small gestures, but ones that we feel bode well for the future.

This work has attempted to explore and, in the process, unveil a certain face of the Muslim patient hitherto hidden from the view of many. We have, with the help of our co-authors, tried to provide healthcare professionals with the key that allows access to the essence, or *qalb*, of the Muslim's being. And if we have succeeded, to whatever extent, we have, we believe, contributed to the breaking of the most important of barriers and the building of the most crucial of bridges.

What comes from the lips reaches the ears.
What comes from the heart reaches the heart.[53]

References and notes

1 Hugo of St Victor *Eruditio didascalia*. Cited in: Nasr SH (1997) *Man and Nature: the spiritual crisis in modern man*, p 10. ABC, Chicago.

2 Macpherson W (1999) *Report for the Stephen Lawrence Inquiry*. The Stationery Office, London.

3 Straw J (1999) *House of Commons Hansand Debates*, 24 February, col 391. HMSO, London.

4 Ahmad WIU (1993) *'Race' and Health in Contemporary Britain*. OUP, Buckingham.

5 Parkin D (1999) Suffer many healers. In: JR Hinnells, R Porter (eds) *Religion, health and suffering*, p 434. Kegan Paul, London.

6 Bacon F (1995) In: T Anderson (ed) *The New Organon*. Bobbs Merrill, Indianapolis.

7 Russell BA (1979) *A History of Western Philosophy*. Allen and Unwin, London.

8 Butt N (1991) *Science and Muslim Societies*. Grey Seal, London.

9 Porter R (1970) *The Greatest Benefit to Mankind*, pp 270–396. Harper Collins, London.

10 Foucault M (1973) *The Birth of the Clinic*. Tavistock, London.

11 Medline literature search by the authors using the search term 'battle' retrieved 1060 articles for the period 1990–October 1999.

12 Runnymede Trust (1997) *Islamophobia: a challenge for us all*. Runnymede Trust, London.

13 Gunny A (1996) *Images of Islam: eighteenth century writings*. Grey Seal, London.

14 Thomson A (1989) *Blood on the Cross*. Ta Ha, London.

15 Eaton G (1985) *Islam and the Destiny of Man*, pp 9–30. George Allen and Unwin, London.

16 Esposito JL (1992) *The Islamic Threat*. OUP, Oxford.

17 Qureshi B (1989) *Transcultural Medicine*. Kluwer, London.

18 Leff J (1988) *Psychiatry Around the Globe: a transcultural view*. Gaskell Press, Penguin, London.

19 Littlewood R, Lipsedge M (1982) *Aliens and Alienists: ethnic minorities and psychiatry*. Penguin, London.

20 Helman CG (1994) *Culture, Health and Illness*. Butterworth-Heinemann, Oxford.

21 Sheikh A (1999) Religion, health and suffering. *J R Soc Med*. **92**: 600–1.

22 Zyst KG (1993) *Religious Medicine: the history and evolution of Indian medicine*. Transaction Publishers, New Brunswick.

23 Unschuld P (1985) *Medicine in China: a history of ideas*. University of California Press, Berkeley.

24 Bray F (1997) Chinese health beliefs. In: JR Hinnells, R Porter (eds) *Religion, Health and Suffering*, pp 187–211. Kegan Paul, London.

25 Singer C, Underwood EA (1962) *A Short History of Medicine*. Clarendon Press, Oxford.

26   Nasr SH (1997) *Man and Nature: the spiritual crisis in modern man.* ABC, Chicago.

27   Nasr SH (1997) *The Need for a Sacred Science.* Curzon Press, Richmond.

28   Sloan RP, Bagiella P, Powell T (1999) Religion, spirituality and medicine. *Lancet.* **353**: 664–7.

29   King DE, Bushwick B (1994) Beliefs and attitudes of hospital inpatients about faith healing and prayer. *J Fam Pract.* **39**: 349–52.

30   Koenig HG (1999) Religion and medicine. *Lancet.* **353**: 1803.

31   Koenig HG, George LK, Cohen HJ, Hays JC, Larson DB, Blazer DG (1998) The relationship between religious activities and cigarette smoking in older adults. *J Gerontol A Biol Sci Med Sci.* **53**: M426–34.

32   Koenig HG, George LK, Meador KG, Blazer DG, Ford SM (1994) Religious practices and alcoholism in a southern adult population. *Hosp Commun Psychiat.* **45**: 225–31.

33   Strawbridge WJ, Cohen RD, Shema SJ, Kaplan GA (1997) Frequent attendance at religious services and mortality over 28 years. *Am J Public Hlth.* **87**: 957–61.

34   King DE, Hueston W, Rudy M (1994) Religious affiliation and obstetric outcome. *South Med J.* **87**: 1125–8.

35   Koenig HG, George LK, Hays JC, Larson DB, Cohen HJ, Blazer DG (1998) The relationship between religious activities and blood pressure in older adults. *Int J Psychiatry Med.* **28**: 189–213.

36   Rabin BS (1999) Religion and medicine. *Lancet.* **353**: 1803.

37   Hummer RA, Rogers RG, Nam CB, Elison CG (1999) Religious involvement and US adult mortality. *Demography.* **36**: 273–85.

38   Koenig HG, Hays JC, Larson DB, *et al.* (1999) A six year follow-up study of 3968 older adults. *J Gerontol A Biol Sci Med Sci.* **54**: M370–6.

39   Oman D, Reed D (1998) Religion and mortality among the community dwelling elderly. *Am J Public Hlth.* **88**: 1469–75.

40   Kark JD, Shemi G, Friedlander Y, Martin O, Manor O, Blondheim SH (1996) Does religious observance promote health? Secular vs kibbutzim in Israel. *Am J Public Hlth.* **86**: 341–6.

41   Koenig HG, Larson DB (1998) Use of hospital services, religious attendance, and religious affiliation. *South Med J.* **91**: 925–32.

42   Sicher F, Targ E, Moore D, Smith HJ (1998) A randomised double-blind study of the effects of distant healing in a population with advanced AIDS. Report of a small-scale study. *West J Med.* **169**: 356–63.

43   Department of Health (1999) *The Patient's Charter.* DoH, London.

44   General Medical Council (1995) *Duties of a Doctor.* GMC, London.

45   Hancock C (1999) Foreword. In: A Henley, J Schott (eds) *Culture, Religion and Patient Care in a Multi-ethnic Society.* Age Concern England, London.

46   Anon (1998) Faith, health and communities. *Our Healthier Nation Target.* **31**: 2–4.

47   Matthews DA, Larson DB (1997) Faith and medicine: reconciling the twin traditions of healing. *Mind/body Med.* **2**: 3–6.

48 HRH The Prince of Wales (1993) *Islam and the West*. Speech delivered in Oxford, 27 October.

49 The Right Honourable Tony Blair MP (1999) *Fighting for a society of shared values and human dignity*. Speech delivered in London, 5 May.

50 The Right Honourable Robin Cook MP (1998) *A new dialogue with Islam*. Speech delivered in London, 8 October.

51 Fatchett D (1999) Strengthening relationships between Islam and the West. *The Muslim News.* **117**: 12.

52 The Right Honourable Frank Dobson MP (1998) Speaking at the Muslim Doctors and Dentists Association and The Islamic Medical Association of North America Annual Conference in Birmingham, 27 June.

53 Arab proverb. Cited in: Ahmed AS (1993). *Living Islam*, p 211. BBC Books, London.

Appendices and Glossary

APPENDIX ONE

Islam and medicine on the World Wide Web

Matlub Hussain

This guide aims to allow quick and easy access to high-quality material of potential relevance to the care of Muslim patients from the World Wide Web (WWW). Those with limited experience in accessing health-related resources from the web are advised to begin with 'Getting Started' (Section 1), a generic introduction to searching the web, followed by a brief compendium of some of the most useful health resources available on-line. More experienced surfers may wish to start with 'Islam and Muslims' (Section 2), a diverse array of sites allowing an authoritative and detailed insight into the religion of one-fifth of humanity. 'Muslim Health Resources' (Section 3) allows access to practical information that institutions and professionals involved in the care of Muslim patients should find useful.

Where possible, web sites have been evaluated using the criteria suggested by Kim *et al.*, assessing sites by their design, aesthetics, content, accessibility and quality of site maintenance, while also taking into consideration the site's policy on disclosing potential conflicts of interest.[1]

Web Site Ready Reckoner

*	Not worth wasting time with
**	Some useful material
***	Good
****	Well worth a visit
*****	Can't afford to miss this site

Section 1:   Getting started

- **ABC of medical computing** ***

  www.bmjpg.com/data/abcmc.htm

  Based on the popular *British Medical Journal* series, this site provides a clear and user-friendly introduction to the world of medical computing. An ideal starting point.

- **Department of Health** *****

  http://www.doh.gov.uk/dhhome.htm

  New Labour's commitment to 'open government' has resulted in this practical site allowing access to authoritative and up-to-date information directly from the Department of Health (DoH). Read recent DoH circulars, press releases and key publications on-line. The compendium of current NHS research programmes is particularly useful for researchers and those involved with health policy development.

- **European Commission** ***

  http://europa.eu.int/comm/index_en.htm

  As European integration continues to gather pace, The European Commission is set to play an increasingly important role in determining health policy. Log in regularly to keep abreast of the latest developments. This site should also be of interest to health services researchers providing ready access to research funding opportunities through the CORDIS (Community Research and Development Information Service) agency.

- **Health Authority** ****

  http://www.hea.org.uk

  A well-developed site from the UK's leading health promotion agency. The Health Authority is committed to reducing health inequalities.

- **He@lth information on the Internet** ****

  http://www.wellcome.ac.uk/healthinfo/

  A Royal Society of Medicine and Wellcome Trust collaborative venture that allows easy and efficient navigation of the millions of pages dedicated to health on the WWW.

- **Hotmail** ****

  http://lc3.law5.hotmail.passport.com/cgi-bin/login

  Set up a personal WWW-based electronic mail account – free of charge – allowing access to email from anywhere in the world.

- **Kings Fund introduction to IT and multimedia** ****

  http://www.kingsfund.org.uk/multit/default.htm

  A brief but authoritative introduction to information technology (IT), detailing its relation and potential to healthcare provision. A useful glossary of key IT terminology is provided.

- **National Library of Medicine** *****

  http://www.nlm.nih.gov/

  For those interested in searching the biomedical literature this site remains the first port of call. Funded by the US Government, it allows free access to Medline, CancerNet and many other important databases.

- **World Health Organisation** *****

  www.who.ch/

  An easy-to-use site that provides reliable information on issues relating to global healthcare (e.g. population control strategies, national immunisation policies and female circumcision). Well worth a visit for those interested in 'the wider picture'.

- **Yahoo** *****

  www.yahoo.com/

  One of the best web search engines available. Simple and easy to use, Yahoo allows instantaneous access to information on the subject of your choice from anywhere in cyberspace. A personal favourite and well worth book-marking!

Section 2:   Islam and Muslims

- **BBC World Service: Islam** ****

  http://www.bbc.co.uk/worldservice/religion/islam/beliefs.htm

  An excellent summary of the essentials of Islam on one web page. Allows for audio-downloads of BBC World Service broadcasts on Islam.

- **Cyber Mosque** ****

  http://atschool.eduweb.co.uk/sirrobhitch.suffolk/mosque/default.htm

  Many Muslims will visit a Mosque several times each day for their daily prayers. This virtual Mosque tour allows one to begin to appreciate its appeal.

- **Discover Islam** *****

  www.discoverislam.com/

  A picture is worth a thousand words, as demonstrated by this gallery of 25 posters masterfully integrating traditional Islamic art and the latest in computer graphics to give an accurate overview of Islam.

- **Holy Qur'an Browser** *****

  http://goon.stg.brown.edu/quran_browser/pqeasy.shtml

  A database developed by the Brown University Scholarly Technology Group that allows fast and reliable key word searches of the primary text of Islamic Law.

- **Images of Islam** *****

  http://www.ummah.org.uk/sanders/

  Breathtaking images captured during a lifetime of travel through the Muslim heartland. A must-visit site!

- **Islam city** ****

  http://islam.org/

  All you wanted to know about Islam but were afraid to ask! This is the major Islamic portal providing a good overview of Islam, broadcast of prayers from Mecca, and more! The site of choice for the BBC, CNN and ABC broadcasting corporations.

- **Islamic interlink** ****

  http://www.ais.org/~islam

  A compendium of Muslim sites on the WWW; its user-friendly interface makes it a real winner.

- **Muslim Council of Britain** ***

  http://www.mcb.org.uk

  An umbrella group that represents over 250 Muslim organisations across Britain. Useful for those interested in keeping abreast of Muslim current affairs.

- **Muslim demographics** ***

  http://websolution.net/islamicweb/population.htm

  A summary and world map – based on United Nations data – of the ethnic and geographic distribution of the Muslim peoples.

- **Muslims in Britain** ****

  http://news2.thls.bbc.co.uk/hi/english/special%5Freport/1997/religion/newsid%5F33000/33539.stm

  A special report by the BBC News online team on what it means to be a Muslim in Britain.

Section 3:   Muslim health resources

*   **Cyber Hajj** *****

    www.islam.org/cybertv/ch18.htm

    A feast of multimedia downloads from ABC and CNN News channels that takes you on a virtual pilgrimage to Mecca – you'll think you are actually there! Very usefully complements Chapter 7, Hajj: journey of a lifetime, illustrating not only the importance of the journey but also the potential health risks pilgrims face.

*   **Direction of prayer** ***

    http://arabia.com/prayer.html

    Muslims pray facing towards Mecca – now easily determined for any of the major world cities using this handy database. Practical help for the Muslim patient in hospital who may wish to pray.

*   **How to perform ablution and prayer** ***

    http://wings.buffalo.edu/sa/muslim/library/salah/index.html

    This well-illustrated site provides valuable information for healthcare professionals who may need to help a patient perform ablution (*Wudu*) or prayer.

*   **International Institute of Islamic Medicine** **

    http://www.iiim.org/

    Aims to promote Islamic medicine globally.

*   **IPCI** ***

    http://www.ipci-iv.co.uk/

    This charity allows hospitals to order copies of the Holy Qur'an free of charge.

- **Islamic culture and medical arts** ****

  http://www.nlm.nih.gov/exhibition/islamic_medical/islamic_00.html

  Emilie Savage Smith of the University of Oxford gives an intriguing account of the intricate relationship between medicine and culture in the Islamic worldview. Read her book on-line, courtesy of the National Library of Medicine.

- **Islamic Medical Association of South Africa** ****

  http://www.ima.org.za/

  The most well-organised Islamic Medical Association on the WWW. A number of important titles (e.g. *Islamic Medical Ethics*) can be ordered directly from this site.

- **Islamic mind body medicine** ****

  http://naqshbandi.org/frmteach.htm

  Many of those trained in the biomedical model of medicine are gradually beginning to appreciate the merits of complementary medical techniques. Islamic spiritual healing practices are discussed in this multimedia lecture delivered at the Harvard Medical School – ancient wisdom in a modern world. (Click on the Suhba section.)

- **Muslim traveller** ****

  www.cdc.gov/travel/travel.html

  Many pilgrims choose to travel to their country of origin before returning to Britain. The Centre for Diseases Control provides accurate and authoritative travel information via an attractive and easy to use interface.

- **Organ donation** ***

  www.worldserver.pipex.com/coi/depts/GDH/coi1568b.ok

  The landmark Fatwa (religious verdict) by the UK Muslim Law Council encouraging Muslims to organ donate, made available on-line courtesy of the DoH. Useful material for transplant teams faced with Muslims who may be apprehensive about organ donation or transplantation on religious grounds.

- **Prayer timetable** **

  http://salam.muslimsonline.com/~salat/salat.cgi

  Gives prayer times for the major world cities.

- **St Bartholomew's and London Hospital Islamic Society** ****

  http://www.mds.qmw.ac.uk/student/islamic/

  Maps of prayer facilities in several London teaching hospitals. Of considerable benefit to patients and hospital visitors who would like to pray.

- **The Muslim patient** ***

  http://pw1.netcom.com/~etori/muslim-pt.html

  An on-line copy of the leaflet 'The Muslim Patient' distributed by the American Muslim Foundation. Aims at equipping healthcare professionals with information of importance in the day-to-day care of Muslim patients.

- **UK Mosque database** **

  http://www.ummah.org/mosques/

  Greater co-operation between religious leaders and health providers would surely allow health promotion and healthcare provision to be more sensitively and effectively delivered. This database allows local Mosques and religious leaders to be easily traced.

Reference

1   Kim P, Eng TR, Deering MJ, Maxfield A (1999) Published criteria for evaluating health related web sites: review. *BMJ*. **318**: 647–9.

Muslim organisations

Matlub Hussain and Sangeeta Dhami

Umbrella organisations

Association of Muslim Schools
1 Evington Lane, Leicester LE5 5PQ
Tel: 0116 273 8666
Fax: 0116 273 8777

Federation of Students Islamic Societies
38 Mapesbury Road, London NW2 4JD
Tel: 020 8452 4493
Fax: 020 8208 4161
Email: fosis@fosis.demon.co.uk

Muslim Council of Britain
PO Box 52, Wembley, Middlesex HA9 0XW
Tel: 020 8903 9024
Fax: 020 8903 9026
Email: admin@mcb.org.uk

Union of Muslim Organisations
109 Campden Hill Road, London W8 7TL
Tel: 020 7229 0538
Fax: 020 7792 2130

Key mosques

England

Council of Mosques
6 Clarmont, Bradford BD7 1 6Q
Tel: 01274 732 479
Fax: 01274 660928

Islamic Cultural Centre
146 Park Road, London NW8 7RG
Tel: 020 7724 3363–7
Fax: 020 7724 0493

UK Islamic Mission
202 North Gower Street, London NW1 2LY
Tel: 020 7380 0465
Fax: 020 7383 0867
Email: ukim@centraloffice.freeserve.com.uk

Scotland

Glasgow Islamic Centre and Central Mosque
Mosque Avenue, Gorbals, Glasgow G5 9TX
Tel: 0141 4293132

Wales

South Wales Islamic Centre
Alice Street, Butetown, Cardiff CF1 5LB
Tel: 029 20460243

Northern Ireland

Belfast Islamic Centre
38 Wellington Park, Belfast BT9 6DN
Tel: 028 90682755

Muslim institutes

International Institute of Islamic Thought
40 London House, 253 Lower Mortlake Road
Richmond, Surrey TW9 2UD
Tel: 020 8948 5166
Fax: 020 8940 4014

Islamic Academy
23 Metcalfe Road, Cambridge CB4 2DB
Tel: 01223 350976

Islamic Foundation
Markfield Dawah Centre
Ratby Lane, Markfield, Leicester LE67 9RN
Tel: 01530 244944
Fax: 01530 244946
(*Note:* The Education and Training Unit of the Islamic Foundation has
been running cultural awareness courses since 1991.)

Muslim Educational Trust
130 Stroud Green Road, London N4 3RZ
Tel: 020 7272 8502
(*Note:* The Muslim Educational Trust has a particular interest in the
subject of sex education for Muslim children.)

Muslim Institute
6 Endsleigh Road, London WC1H 0DS
Tel: 020 7388 2581

Oxford Centre for Islamic Studies
St Cross College, Oxford OX1 3TO
Tel: 01865 725077

Women's organisations

An-Nisa Society
Bestways Complex, 2 Abbey Road, London NW10 7BW
Tel: 020 8838 0311
(*Note:* An-Nisa Society has pioneered several highly successful projects
covering the themes of sexual health education, sexual abuse, and
adoption and fostering.)

Muslim Women's Helpline
11 Main Drive, GEC East Lane Estate, Wembley, Middlesex HA9 7PX
Tel: 020 8904 8193
(*Note:* Voluntary organisation offering confidential telephone
counselling, support and help to Muslim women. Timings: Monday to
Friday 10 am–4 pm.)

Miscellaneous

Association of Muslims with Disabilities (UK)
1 Hawthorn Road, London NW10 2NE
Tel/Fax: 020 8830 3821

Islamic Shariah Council
34 Francis Road, London E10 6BW
Tel/Fax: 020 8881 3984

Muslim Directory
65A Grosvenor Road, London W7 1HR
Tel: 020 8840 0020
Fax: 020 8840 8819
Email: info@muslimdirectory.co.uk
(*Note:* A reasonably comprehensive directory of Muslim organisations
and businesses in the UK.)

Muslim Doctors and Dentists Association
311 Burbury Street, Birmingham B19 1TT
Tel: 0121 551 9931

Muslim Marriage Guidance Council
The Brighton Islamic Mission
8 Caburn Road, Hove, Sussex BN3 6ET
Tel: 01273 722 438
Fax: 01273 279439

Glossary

Abtest: Turkish term for the ritual ablution that precedes the five daily prayers (*see Wudu*).

Adhan: the call to prayer. Within this call are incorporated the basic tenets of Islam – the belief that Allah alone is worthy of worship and that Muhammad is the Messenger of Allah. The call concludes with the reminder that true felicity is dependent on the realisation of this basic truth. It is customary to whisper the words of the Adhan into the right ear of the newborn immediately after birth.

Afiya: a state of wholeness and totality.

Allah: the Supreme Being. The term Allah is unique in that it does not have any gender connotation and does not allow a plural form.

Aqiqah: the celebratory sacrifice of a sheep on the birth of a child. The meat is distributed between family members and the poor.

Assalamu-Alaikum: peace be with you. The greeting used among Muslims when greeting their living or their dead. It is customary to reciprocate this prayer.

Bimaristan: used to describe both fixed and mobile hospitals. (*Maristan*: hospital for the insane.)

Dhikr: the remembrance of Allah.

Eid: the major days of celebration of the Islamic calendar. *Eid-ul-Fitr* is the festival that follows the Ramadan fast, falling on the 1st of Shawwal. *Eid-ul-Adha* is the festival of sacrifice that coincides with the last day of the Hajj. This occurs on the 10th of Dhul Hijjah.

Fatwa: a formal religious edict.

Fitra: the innate state of purity and goodness with which humans enter this world.

Ghusl: purificatory wash that needs to be taken after ejaculation, sexual intercourse and the end of menstruation.

Hajj (Hadj): the annual pilgrimage to The Sacred Mosque in Mecca is required of all Muslims once in a lifetime. There is an exemption for those with poor health or inadequate finances. (*Hajji*: honorific title given to pilgrims.)

Hadith: the sayings of the Prophet Muhammad.

Hajji: pilgrim. An honorific title given to those who have completed the Hajj.

Halal: all that is lawful, as decreed by Allah. The basic maxim is that 'all is allowed save that which is prohibited'.

Hammam: communal bathing area, particularly common in Turkey.

Imam: religious teacher. Also used to describe the one who leads the daily congregational prayers.

Iqamah: the second call to prayer immediately preceding the prayer itself.

Iqra: to read. The first word of the Qur'an to be revealed.

Islam: literally the act of submitting oneself to the will of Allah through a conscious and voluntary act. The religion of the Muslims.

Istinja: washing one's genitals with free-flowing water after urinating or evacuating. An essential pre-requisite before the daily prayers.

Ka'bah: The Sacred Mosque in Mecca, Saudi Arabia, towards which Muslims will face in their daily prayers.

Muslim: one who has freely and consciously submitted to the will of Allah.

Namaz: used by Muslims from the Indian subcontinent for *Salah* (*see below*).

Qalb: the very essence of a thing. Used to denote both the physical and metaphysical heart. Derived from the verb *yan qalibo* meaning 'to turn'.

Qiblah: the direction of The Sacred Mosque in Mecca. Faces east southeast of Britain.

Qur'an: Allah's final revelation to Man, and the primary source of Islamic Law. Previous revelations have included The Psalms of David, The Torah of Moses and The Gospel of Jesus.

Ramadan: the ninth month of the Islamic calendar and the month in which all adult Muslims are required to fast. Fasting involves a complete abstinence from food and drink during daylight hours. An exemption exists for the elderly, the infirm, and menstruating, pregnant or lactating women.

Sabr: steadfastness, resilience, fortitude, patience and gratitude to Allah at all times, and in all situations.

Salah: the obligatory prayer performed by Muslims five times a day.

Salim: one who is healthy. (*Salama*: safety.)

Salla 'Llahu alayhi wa-sallam: the sending of salutations on the Prophet. An appendage used by the devout whenever they make mention of Muhammad.

Sawm: fasting during the month of Ramadan. An obligation on all sane, healthy adults.

Shahadah: the testimony of faith: 'There is no deity other than Allah; Muhammad is the Messenger of Allah'.

Shariah: the moral, social and legal code of Islam. The primary sources of Shariah are The Qur'an and the body of Prophetic teachings comprising the *Sunnah* (*see below*).

Shifa: a cure or healing. One of the names of Allah is *as-Shafi* meaning 'The Supreme Healer'.

Shi'is (plural **Shi'ia**): distinguished from the mainstream community after the Prophet's death on the basis of their conviction that his descendants alone should be the successors to his temporal authority.

Sufi: pursuing a spiritual path under the direct guidance of a Master.

Sunnah: literally, a path. The pattern of conduct of the Prophet Muhammad comprising his sayings, practices and sanctioned customs.

Sunni: the main body of Muslims representing over 90% of the total Muslim community.

Tahneek: the Prophetic practice of rubbing a small piece of softened date into the upper palate of the newborn.

Taweeez: an amulet containing prayers or sections from the Qur'an.

Tayammum: dry ablution involving wiping the hands and face with dust; a dispensation for those in whom the more usual wet ablution (*see Wudu*) is problematic or may be injurious to health.

Ulema: literally, 'the learned'. Those chosen by the community and charged with the responsibility of formulating Islamic Law using the principles enshrined within the Qur'an and Sunnah.

Umrah: a 'lesser' Pilgrimage to The Scared Mosque performed outside of the Hajj season.

Wudu: ritual ablution that precedes the daily canonical prayers. Involves washing, in sequence, the hands, face, arms and feet.

Zakat: alms tax made payable by all those who have savings above a minimum level at the rate of $2^{1}/_{2}\%$ on annual savings.

Index

ablution *see wudu*
abortion 68
Abraham 17–19, 24, 90
abtest 20, 133
acculturation 37
Adhan 59–60, 133
adoption 68
afiya 36, 133
age profile 8
Allah 18, 22–6, 31, 74, 133
Aqiqah 62, 133
Arabic 36
Assalamu-Alaikum 26, 36, 105, 133

Bangladeshis
  breastfeeding 66
  employment statistics 9–10
  household size 8
  housing 10–11
  naming systems 64
  sex ratio 7–8
  size of British community 4–6
bereavement 97, 101–6
  see also death
bimaristan 35, 133
birth customs 57, 59–62
  Adhan 59–60
  Aqiqah 62
  circumcision 60–2
  shaving the hair 62
  Tahneek 60
  Taweez 60
body, rights of 34
breastfeeding 65–6
  during Ramadan 80
  weaning 66–7
burial 100

Census data 5–6
children
  adoption 68

fostering 68–9
handicapped children 67–8
rights of 58
circumcision 60–2
  female 52
clitoris removal 52
community facilities 12–13
congenital abnormalities 67–8
consanguinity 49–50, 67
contact lenses, *Hajj* and 95
contraception 53
  Hajj and 51, 94–5
  intra-uterine contraceptive device
    (IUCD) 53
Council of Mosques 12

dawa 36
de-infibulation 52–3
death 97, 98
  death rites 100–1
  euthanasia 98
  organ transplants 107
  post-mortems 106–7
  suicide 98
  see also bereavement; dying patients
dehydration during fasting 80
demographics 4–9
  age profile 8
  gender 7–8
  geographical distribution 9
  household size 8
  size of British Muslim community 4–7
dhikr 33, 133
diabetes, fasting and 81
dietary rules 25–6
discrimination 10, 13, 112–13
disease 29
dress 23
dying patients 97, 99–100
  see also death

educational issues 11–12
  medical education 35
Eid ul-Adha 21, 133
Eid ul-Fitr 21, 133
employment statistics 9–10
  female employment 9–10
euthanasia 98
extended families 44–5
  challenges to 45–6

family life 44–8
  extended families 44–5
    challenges to 45–6
  gender issues 46–8
    role demarcation 47–8
    segregation 46–7
  marriage 48–50
    consanguinity 49–50, 67
fasting 73–85
  fast of Ramadan 74–6
  exemptions from 76–7
  meaning of fasting 74–5
  rules of fasting 75–6
  health and 76–81
    case studies 83–5
    implications for health 79–81
    medical exemptions 76–7
    medication use 77–9
    organisational considerations 82–3
    epidemiology of fasting 82
    hospital attendance 82
    primary care 82–3
Fatwa 106, 107, 133
female employment 9–10
female genital tract mutilation
    (FGM) 51–3
fitra 30, 133
five pillars of faith 18–22
fostering 68–9

gender issues 46–8
  role demarcation 47–8
  segregation 46–7
  sex ratio 7–8
geographical distribution of Muslim
    population 9
ghusl 20, 133

Hadith 106, 133
hair, shaving of 62
Hajj 18–19, 21, 22, 89–96, 133
  health risks 91–5
    general advice 95
    infectious diseases 93–4
    menstruation 94–5
    sun and heat 91–3
    travel consultation 95
  on behalf of deceased 106
  rites of 91
  significance of 90
Hajji 133
halal 26, 34, 134
Hammam 24, 134
handicapped children 67–8
health 29
healthcare development 34–5
heart
  healing of 33
  states of 31–3
heat exhaustion/heat stroke risks during
    Hajj 92–3
household size 8
housing 10–11
humanity 23–4

identity 14
illness 31–3
  exemption from fasting 76–7
  terminal illness 99–100
imam 21, 134
infectious disease risks during *Hajj* 93–4
infibulation 52
insecurity 13
intermarriage 49–50
Internet resources *see* World Wide Web
    (WWW) resources
intra-uterine contraceptive device (IUCD)
    53
Iqamah 59, 134
iqra 134
Islam 17–18, 134
  five pillars of faith 18–22
  human condition 23–4
  way of Muhammad 24–7
  Western understanding of 111–13

Islamic Foundation 12
istinja 20, 134

Ka'bah 90, 134

man, essence of 30
maristan 35, 133
marriage 48–50
  consanguinity 49–50, 67
Mecca 18, 89, 90, 100
  see also Hajj
medical education 35
medical ethics 35
medications
  advice relating to *Hajj* 95
  use during fasting 77–9
meningitis outbreak following *Hajj* 93–4
menstruation 50–1
  Hajj and 95
migration to Britain 4
mosques 12
  key mosques 130
  Sacred Mosque 89, 90
  see also Hajj
mourning 104–5
Muhammad 17–18, 20, 22, 24–7, 74, 90
Muslim 134
Muslim Council of Britain (MCB) 12
Muslim Education Trust 12
Muslim organisations 12, 129–32
  key mosques 130
  Muslim institutes 131
  umbrella organisations 129
  women's organisations 131–2
myth of return 4

Namaz 20, 134
names 62–5
  choosing a name 62–3
  naming systems 64–5
  recognising Muslim names 65
National Muslim Education Council of
    the UK 12

organ transplants 107
organisations *see* Muslim organisations

Pakistanis
  consanguinity 49
  employment statistics 9–10
  household size 8
  housing 10–11
  naming systems 64
  sex ratio 7–8
  size of British community 4–6
peptic ulcers during Ramadan 80
periods *see* menstruation
physical state 34–5
  healthcare development 34–5
  rights of the body 34
Pilgrimage *see Hajj*
political participation 13
post-mortems 106–7
prayer timetable 100
pregnancy
  infibulation and 52
  mourning and 105
prejudice 13, 112–13
promiscuity 50

qalb 30, 31, 134
qalb marid 32
qalb salim 32
Qiblah 90, 134
Qur'an 33, 36, 99, 102, 106, 134
Qur'anic framework 36

Ramadan 21–2, 74–6, 134
  implications for health 79–81
  meaning of fasting 74–5
  preparation for 74
  rules of fasting 75–6
    exemptions 76–7
  see also fasting
religion
  health benefits of 114
  respect for 114–15

Sabr 102–3, 134
Sacred Mosque 89, 90
  see also Hajj
Salah 20–2, 134
salim 31–2, 134

salla 'Llahu alayhi wa-sallam 25, 134
Sarwar, Mohammed 13
sawm 134
segregation of the sexes 46–7
sex ratio 7–8
sexuality 23
    contraception 53
    sexual norms 50
Shahada 22, 135
Shariah 107, 135
shaving the hair 62
shifa 33, 34, 135
Shi'is 26, 135
sickness *see* illness
sleep patterns during Ramadan 79
socio-economics 9–14
    community facilities 12–13
    educational issues 11–12
    employment statistics 9–10
    housing 10–11
    identity 14
    insecurity 13
    political participation 13
sufi 135
suicide 98
sunburn risks during *Hajj* 92
sunnah 25, 26, 135
Sunnis 26, 135

Tahneek 60, 135
Taweez 60, 135

tayammum 20, 135
terminal illness 99–100
termination of pregnancy 68
travel consultation 95

Ulema 135
Umrah 89, 135
unemployment 10
Union of Muslim Organisations in
        the United Kingdom and
        Eire (UMO) 12
United Kingdom Islamic Mission 12

vaccinations, *Hajj* and 94

weaning 66–7
women
    employment 9–10
    role demarcation 47–8
    segregation 46–7
    status of 46
women's organisations 131–2
World Wide Web (WWW)
        resources 121–8
    general resources 122–4
    Islam and Muslim sites 124–5
    Muslim health resources 126–8
wudu 20, 135

Zakat 22, 135